MINISTRY

The Nuts and Bolts of Church Administration

Thomas F. Tumblin

Abingdon Press
Nashville

ADMINISTRY:
THE NUTS AND BOLTS OF CHURCH ADMINISTRATION

Copyright © 2017 by Thomas F. Tumblin

Library of Congress Cataloging-in-Publication Data has been requested.

ISBN 978-1-4267-2700-9

Scripture quotations unless noted otherwise are from the Common English Bible. Copyright © 2011 by the Common English Bible. All rights reserved. Used by permission. www.CommonEnglishBible.com.

Scripture quotations marked (NRSV) are taken from the New Revised Standard Version of the Bible, copyright 1989, Division of Christian Education of the National Council of the Churches of Christ in the United States of America. Used by permission. All rights reserved.

Scripture quotations marked (KJV) are taken from The Authorized (King James) Version. Rights in the Authorized Version in the United Kingdom are vested in the Crown. Reproduced by permission of the Crown's patentee, Cambridge University Press.

17 18 19 20 21 22 23 24 25 26—10 9 8 7 6 5 4 3 2 1
MANUFACTURED IN THE UNITED STATES OF AMERICA

AD
MINISTRY

CONTENTS

PREFACE

One of the miracles of God's grace is the entrusting of ministry into the hands of mere mortals. When Peter received Christ's instructions accompanying the keys of the kingdom of heaven, he could no longer plead ignorance. In good levitical tradition, the divine trust passed from the Messiah to the Messiah's agents. Authority was vested with the assignment. How we manage ministry on earth has some type of mystical connection to God's actions in heaven. And as we mimic God's heavenly intent, grace will flow on earth.

In the context of a local congregation, that trust carries a set of expectations. We do not simply enjoy the authority of heaven. We bear responsibility to shepherd God's people and witness to our neighborhoods around the world. Just as God came on a mission through Jesus Christ, we are on a missional journey making visible the kingdom of God. What ministry we do, and how we do it, matters.

In the following pages we will explore the nuts and bolts of ministry— the administry of the church. Where two or three are gathered together, there Christ shows up. So also do the seeds of systems and structures that govern life together as a Christian community. Should the two or three expand to two or three hundred, ministry becomes rather complex. Where will they meet? Who will lead and how? What would a fair wage be for those leading the congregation? What are the regional legal considerations for such a large assembly? How will members be mobilized to fulfill their own call to ministry? How will they have a clear sense of direction and purpose?

Not every pastor or faithful lay leader will resonate with the tools we discuss. Some would prefer to focus on preaching or pastoral care. Others will tend toward teaching or social outreach. The flesh and muscles of incarnational ministry require a skeleton. The tools discussed will include budgets, strategies, personnel, legalities, and facilities as means to the end of faithful mission. Consider this book a primer for these critical and complex domains of administry.

I want to acknowledge the expert insights of Mrs. Barbara Antrobus, executive director of human resources, and Mr. Bryan Blankenship, vice president of finance and administration at Asbury Theological Seminary. They contribute their professional wisdom in our Administrative Issues in Church Leadership course with great style and ease. Their perspectives provided the content check for the chapters on staffing and finances.

Chapter 1

THE GENIUS OF ADMINISTRY

The story is told of a conversation between Rick Warren, founding pastor of Saddleback Community Church in California, and Peter Drucker, the famous organizational scholar. Rick was reflecting on the movemental nature of the congregation and his desire to never allow it to become a dead bureaucracy. He had seen too many effective churches become overgrown and stalled institutions. He intended to keep Saddleback's structure lean to avoid lethargy and eventual demise.

That fear looms for denominations and associations as well as local congregations. Few frustrations rise above the sick feeling of a once flexible and responsive organization that now lumbers along with more rules and regulations than grace and vitality. What began as a fresh expression of hopeful mission can, often without intending to, get hamstrung in complex layers of bureaucracy.

The church as a historic institution is grounded in thousands of years of tradition. Change is expected to be slow in light of such a legacy. The church as a collection of faithful communities, to the contrary, must respond to the ongoing realities of each era. It is called to honor tradition while adapting to how that tradition is lived out contextually. To use one of Christ's analogies, the church must be ready to carry the New Wine of the Spirit in pliable containers.

Hence, the genius of administry. Responsive leaders designing and executing new structures for creative ministry is a beautiful sight. The shift from maintenance to mission through entrepreneurial stewards inspires greater ingenuity. Confidently bounded by the traditions, resourceful administers put oil on existing wineskins to keep them supple while appropriately supplying new vessels for the emerging demands of the setting. They understand new wineskins are best when trying to contain the volatility of active ministry fermentation. Brittle wineskins that can no longer be reconditioned are discarded.

Administry—the coming alongside ministry to help it reach the intended result(s)—mirrors the description of the Holy Spirit in scripture. The third person of the Trinity comes as comforter, empowerer, waymaker. The Spirit does not do hostile takeovers or manipulation. The Holy Spirit animates the character of Christ in believers. Administry helps create pathways for Spirit-powered faithfulness.

In the same way, administry does not seek to overly control. Administry (the term we will use frequently throughout this book for positive administration) animates rather than blindly dictates. It enlivens mission, paving the way for lives to be changed. Administry provides pliable systems and structures that adjust to new contexts and unexpected circumstances. Administry serves ministry—not the other way around.

By the way, Peter Drucker, in hearing Warren's concerns, reminded him that no lasting movement thrives without supporting systems and structures. Too many emerging ministries fail to live beyond one generation. Unless enough organizational infrastructure exists for the movement to live beyond the founder, it will not survive. Those backbone elements must fit the shape of the mission. They need to allow for optimal elasticity. At the same time, they bring form and function to important activities. Every movement requires some ordering.

An Ecology of Administry

Alan Roxburgh and Fred Romanuk illustrate this truth in their book *The Missional Leader*. They adapt research from David Hurst and others that maps a recurring cycle of organizational life. Rather than the typical bell curve that depicts the birth, maturation, and eventual death of an enterprise, these authors assume (correctly) that organizations resist terminatation. In fact, we can all point to examples of companies and associations that lost their vitality decades ago yet continue to act as if they were making significant contributions to society. Organizations are generally tenacious, even if that means looking more like zombies than like healthy influences. The ecology model acknowledges the closed-loop nature of groups and organizations. They are born, and then, if vigorous, they continue to remake themselves.[1]

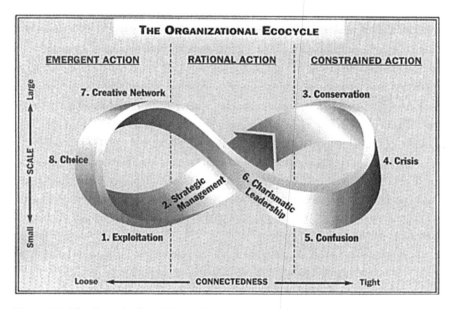

Figure 1.1: The Organizational Ecocycle

By choice, healthy organizations opt to do a new thing. They engage in sufficient risk-taking and visioning to launch a new initiative. Once the initiative gains enough momentum to be practicable, wise organizations tend to put legs under it in the form of systems and structures. What staff support will be required? How many resources, financial and otherwise, are needed? How does this initiative fit in the trajectory of our mission? How will we know it is doing well? These rational queries contribute to the design of feedback systems and oversight. When overdone, they choke the life out of the original vision. What began with inspiration and hope

3

tends toward diminished impact and, possibly, the walking dead. When responsive, they fuel mission.

Adminiministry comes alongside emergent movements and provides systems and structures that accelerate missional influence. When done well, it mitigates against the unsustainable weight of inflexible bureaucracy. It assists in providing new wineskins, reconditioning older wineskins and disposing brittle ones.

George Bullard of the Columbia Partnership adds an overlay to the cyclical nature of organizations. He identifies *vision, inclusion, program, and management* as the four priorities that drive organizational life.[2] When first born, the new initiative rises on the updraft of vision that includes others in a hopeful future. The vision gets operationalized in programming and management systems. At the apex of its effectiveness, all four priorities are strong and contributing. After a while they begin to lose their impact in the same order in which they arose. Vision usually fades first. Then people begin to disengage. Programs wane and management systems do all they can to keep the doors open.

Healthy adminiministry stewards the priorities of the organization by building more choices into the cycle. Crises at the point of highest constraint need not be the norm. Strategic decisions earlier in the sequence can infuse new energy before painful constraints take away opportunities. Here is an illustration.

A local pastor and her team of three laypeople completed the first event in their journey toward renewing the congregation. They knew their role included identifying a key leverage point that, if addressed, would help renew the church. They had listened carefully when the presenter asked them to inventory the strengths of the congregation and the church's existing ministries. The same gap was obvious to all four of them—young families. Children, youth, and older adults were well cared for by multiple offerings of discipleship experiences. Young families, particularly those in their twenties and thirties, could not find a place to connect.

Via multiple conversations with those families and church leadership, the team enlisted three influential young families to lead a new ministry to their peers. They designed an impressive strategy for building relationships, serving needs, and nurturing the families in their walk with Christ. The strategy was embraced by the Administrative Council, matched with some modest funding, and the initiative launched. The congregation made the choice to attend to a ministry gap, and administry decisions were made to give it a fruitful beginning. The need was identified, people were recruited, support was provided, and lives were touched in a new way.

The Individual as Administer

Following are three considerations as we begin this journey. First, when thinking about administry, we must acknowledge that some have more affinity to it than others. In fact, some have the spiritual gift of administration. They likely enjoy administry and seek to hone their administry skills with marked satisfaction. Others may be inclined to do almost anything but administry. (I know one colleague who believes administry undermines being a shepherd to a local congregation.) We are all created and gifted differently.

Also, we each have our own "thinking wavelength." How we do administry will depend on our individual levels of bias toward detail. Some tend toward the fine points, and some toward blue-sky visioning. Others are in between the two poles. Tom Paterson, in his book *Living the Life You Were Meant to Live*, offers the following graphic.[3] The more abstract person is likely to prefer the big picture, while the more concrete person will want clear pathways, implementation facts, and numbers. Accounting tasks favor the concrete person while strategic planning tasks favor the more abstract person.

THINKING WAVELENGTH CONSTRUCT

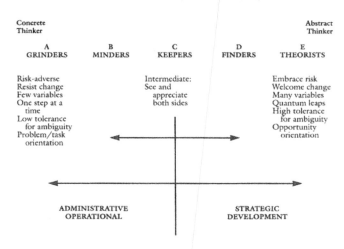

Figure 1.2: Thinking Wavelength Construct

5

No one location on the continuum is better than another. We need each other to realize the full spectrum of abilities in a church or organization. Otherwise, the visionary may drop certain details or detailers will lose sight of the end goal. Just as a diversity of spiritual gifts enriches the body of Christ, so a diversity of thinking wavelengths strengthens organizations.

Third, one's sense of empowerment contributes to the administry discussion. To come alongside ministry assumes sufficient confidence in the value one has to offer. If I believe I will only mess up the ministry by coming alongside, I might avoid doing so. At the same time, if I believe I have a significant contribution to make, I am ready to step in as soon as possible.

Figure 1.3: Personal Power Model

Janet Hagberg suggests that a sense of empowerment is a developmental process, one that requires intentional work. Administers, and the efforts they invest, mature from reflective action. How do I influence people? How much do I depend on my associations with other power individuals or groups (such as the Administrative Board) for my sense of power? What are those occasions when I settle for the short-lived porrage of achievement rather than the birthright of wisdom?[4]

Note that by empowerment I do not mean power plays. Individual empowerment accompanies a maturing sense of self, how one is created in God's image and gifted for kingdom life. Power plays—that is, the use or abuse of power for personal gain—seldom enhance the life of a congregation or parachurch organization. Empowerment as a child of God and contributor to God's mission links to our identity and influences our activity. Called ones follow Christ with heart, mind, soul, and strength by the grace of God through the Holy Spirit.

Robust Traits in Mission

The Apostle Paul provides ample reminders of the ordering of the church as the body of Christ. The grace of God through Jesus draws diverse personalities and backgrounds together to demonstrate the kingdom of God on earth. The "redeemed of the LORD say so" through offering themselves to God's purposes this side of heaven (see Psalms 107:2 NRSV). The image of God in each of us gets expressed through multiple temperaments, strengths, weaknesses, and gifts. These assets might be identified through mentoring, a growing self-awareness, experimentation, or by using various assessment tools. They might include Upper Room Books' *Understanding Spiritual Gifts* study, *StrengthsFinder 2.0*,[5] the Keirsey Temperament Sorter, the Emotional and Social Competency Inventory,[6] or another commonly used resource.

Regardless of the path(s) to insight, we soon discover the variety of traits God provides for the church. Some will be entrusted with very public roles by the Creator, and some will be wired for more "behind the scenes" roles. Some traits will lend themselves to more solitary or contemplative settings, while others will be more oriented toward hands-on ministry with large groups of people. I dedicate a chapter of this book to the function of mobilizing people for mission. For now, know that not all giftings and temperaments lend themselves to the necessary administry of the church. A story might help illustrate the point.

In a large congregation committed to placing gifted people into roles that maximize their ministry assets, a physician volunteers in the church office. When asked why she serves in "pushing paper" instead of in the church's medical clinic, the doctor reports greater fulfillment in copying and assembling materials than in clinic work. (She also cares for a percentage of the church's patients in her profession during office hours.) In a similar way, a banker in the same church, when asked why he does not serve on the finance team, reports a preference for tasks that have a beginning and an ending, such as helping to side a neighborhood home being rehabilitated by the congregation.

A Reminder from Steve Jobs: Enjoy the Journey

The untimely death of Steve Jobs, founder of Apple, NExT, and Pixar, might instruct us as well. Numerous commentators have honored his creative genius. Some wonder if Apple will mimic Disney's malaise after the death of its founder, Walt Disney. Many in the press attempted to summarize the qualities that made Jobs such an impressive entrepreneur.

While he had many facets to his reputation, Jobs embodied the principles of simplicity and work as fun. He was fired from Apple at age thirty and created a new business that eventually accelerated the value of Apple when he returned. He embraced what he loved and had no patience for fools. He was often the brilliant one in the room. Co-workers would wager on who could survive Jobs's exhausting critique of a project. Those who did so successfully were often promoted. He knew creativity flows by removing the barriers to access and calling for user interfaces that made the devices more enjoyable.

His life and philosophy demonstrate some values applicable to church leadership. Each iteration of his products pushed for ease of access and tapped human intuition for ease of use. The iPhone, iPad, and iPod each got smaller and faster. Each appealed to the user's experience of the device and its software.

By the way, Jobs did not invent many of the handhelds we enjoy today. He simply made them better. We are told Microsoft had a prototype tablet device years before the iPad was introduced. They simply could not break through the layers of the organization to bring it to production ahead of Apple.

In the same way, church systems need to come alongside mission to make ministry easier and more fulfilling. Committee meetings and software systems can be redemptive as they facilitate frontline activity. As an end in themselves, they are a waste of time and talent. Staff handbooks and insurance policies are critical for responsible life together, but they are no substitute for vital, life-on-life transformation.

"Prepare Ye the Way"

The chapters that follow introduce the basic functions of administry. Begin with an assessment of current practices. What already exists? Where are processes and activities well aligned and where are some adjustments recommended? How do the values and culture influence the behaviors of the church?

Consider the saints, current and potential, that God has gathered around the mission. Who has God raised up? Are they paid or unpaid? Where are the support systems for their effective growth into Christlikeness? (Yes, work ideally fosters formation.) How will they know expectations and be equipped to fulfill them?

Care for the financial assets. How will the church manage the resources of the congregation? Where do the offerings go, and how will we communicate that they are well stewarded? Who is responsible for budgeting? What is the role of the finance committee?

Honor God's house. What does it mean to be a facilities manager? How much space is enough? What does a maintenance schedule look like? What is the role of the trustees? Should all the work be volunteer?

Walk by faith while managing risk. How much insurance is adequate? What does a safety plan look like? Who is in charge during natural disasters? Who meets with the press? Do we need an attorney? Why incorporate?

Seek God's resources for mission. What is an annual stewardship campaign? How much is enough? What if we decide to raise capital funds?

Are there other sources of income for the local church? Should the church have a side business?

The final chapter invites us to lean into the tension of a spiritual journey steeped in real-world responsibilities, ones that, if not handled well, could land us in court. If administry is coming alongside, how do we live in the both/and of following the Spirit while making a way for mission? What is the best mix of trust and trustworthiness? How does the pastor call the best out of both realists and dreamers?

Welcome to the journey of way-making. You are not traveling alone.

Chapter 2
A REASON FOR BEING

Churches are hard to stop, especially when they are grounded in a clear theological understanding of why they exist. Healthier congregations realize they cannot rely solely on the broad denominational heritage they may enjoy, as rich as the theological underpinnings of that heritage may be. Theology gets worked out in location. Biblical and theological distinctives may be passed down by the founders of a movement, but how that DNA gets expressed is always contextual. United Methodist churches, for example, vary greatly on how they live out their faith in community.

In the same way, the nuances of belief and behavior interact within the characteristics of the setting. Worship in Honolulu, Hawaii, no doubt contrasts with worship in Nome, Alaska. The rubrics might be exactly alike, but the life experiences out of which the worship rises shape the worship encounter. How churches live out ministry varies in similar ways from place to place. Those differences might be related to the state and local regulations. They also relate to how the congregation thinks and acts theologically.

A Theological Model for Adminstry

We have already talked about administration as "coming alongside." Church management is not the primary focus in congregational or institutional life. Administrative activities are not the end of mission. They build and support useful systems for mission. Effectiveness is not measured by the number and length of meetings. Robust mission shows up when the people of God live out the call of God. Unencumbered faithfulness to God's mandate bears the fruit of changed lives.

Historically, the church has been described as one, holy, universal, and apostolic, as summarized in the Nicene Creed. The called-out people of God resemble the character of God in that they embody "one Lord, one faith, one baptism" (Ephesians 4:1-6). With this common Redeemer, all Christ-followers enjoy relationship with the same triune God, albeit in varying expressions of God's life pulsing through them.

This God-life describes the presence of God's Holy Spirit, the promise of God in us. The Spirit draws us into God's transforming grace, animates us in living out God's purpose, and engages us in the journey of holiness. The Spirit comforts, empowers, and converts. By the Holy Spirit, we are changing from one level of Christlikeness to the next. We are becoming holy as God is holy.

God's people over the centuries enjoy an indissoluble bond and participation with the saints of the ages. Just as there is one church in any given era, so believers in all eras are connected in the God who transcends time and space. Worship at 10:30 Sunday morning or in my private devotion joins the worship of the Christ-followers who have gone before and those who will be after me. We are as much of the same body as the African or Asian or Latin American Christian today as we are of the Christian who lived in the second century.

The church's apostolicity points not only to the lineage of the apostles of Christ, particularly the testimony of Peter on which Jesus said he would build his church. It also bears witness to the God who comes. Jesus took on human flesh to make God known. Likewise, we embrace God's mission to make the kingdom of God visible throughout the earth and to every generation. Love compels us to go and make disciples. Since we have received the gift of life abundant in Jesus Christ, we become gift-bearers to all.

Professors Howard A. Snyder and Daniel V. Runyon add to these classical descriptors the creative tensions of the book of Acts and the Gospels.

They describe the church as not only one, but also diverse, both holy and charismatic, universal (catholic) and local (in a given context), and apostolic and prophetic.[1] Our unity shines more brightly because of the multifaceted uniqueness of each individual. Just as the Godhead is Three-in-One, so the church is many-in-One. The church is both set apart for God in holiness while also experiencing the gifting and power of the Holy Spirit. The church both joins the saints throughout the ages while enjoying the qualities and influences of an identifiable time and context. The church not only has good news, but also news of justice and holy fire for its era.

The Church as Organization

But how do we think about the local church as an organization? How do systems, structures, resources, and people relate to one another in God's design? From a Christian perspective, consider the following model.

Figure 2.1: A Theological Model for Administration

All of creation begins and ends with the triune God. As Paul preached on Mars Hill, "In God we live, move and exist" (Acts 17:28). Creation

13

was spoken into existence by God's word and continues to exist only by the patience of a loving Creator. Organizations, as a human phenomenon, are an attempt to bring order and focus to human activity. The church as an organization emerges as God's people relate to one another and to the Lord. The biblical vision of who God is and God's intent for all people draws together, by the Holy Spirit, groups of believers on a mission.

The persons of the Trinity live in perfect harmony, faultless relationship. They are a "community of being" in flawless sync with one another. They do not compete with one another. They do not argue or fight. They do not step on each other's toes. They dance in perfect movement with one another in indescribable beauty. They relate to one another in perfect love and generativity since beauty always elicits creativity.

They are so much in sync that they are both one and three simultaneously, what theologians call *mutual penetration*. At the same time, they are not so unified as to be commingling. The Trinity is three persons in one, not a blend or hybrid. The triune God is so unified as to be one, so distinct as to be three.

As my language illustrates, the triune God is also mystery. How Father, Son, and Holy Spirit relate to one another in the Godhead remains inexplicable to a degree. That quality of mystery draws us in toward wonder and awe.

God's highest creation is humankind. Since we are made in the image of God, we bear the mark of God on our lives. In relationship with God through Jesus Christ, the Spirit resides in us in great power. We bear the triune God. Every human being carries the image of God because we share the same Creator. There are no rankings of one class or race above another. We are "neither Greek nor Jew, . . . male [or] female" as cocreated beings (see Galatians 3:28). Since all of creation yearns for redemption, humanity shares a common hope. In Christ, we can know God and are promised to be in relationship with God forever. What we comprehend with our senses is not permanent, but the Creator is. We are invited into eternal fellowship with the Holy One, who will redeem heaven and earth.

Simultaneously, the metanarrative of scripture speaks of God's missional intent for humanity. Noah, Abraham, the judges, and the prophets accent the covenant arrangement God desires with humankind. Christ's and the apostles' teachings flesh out the purpose of God's search for restored relationship. The Promised One has come and has shown us God's love for every person. New people in a new creation continues to be God's plan.

In the meantime, God's activity occurs in a fallen world. Sin's venom poisons paradise. The intimacy modeled before the serpent's handiwork now equates to seeing in a mirror, dimly (see 1 Corinthians 13:12 NRSV). Evil's fingerprints are all over creation and humanity, resulting in spiritual and environmental deterioration. Men and women carry the burdens of sweat of the brow and pain in childbirth, indicators of the terminal condition of the present world. What we can see, touch, hear, taste, and smell remains imperfect and temporary.

Ultimately, God wins. The order of the day this side of heaven is God's mission of salvation. Grace is at work around the world. The kingdom of God has come and the final implications of God's reign are inevitable. As participants in God's redemptive activity, we enjoy the down payment of the Spirit—God with us now in fullness of life while being the foretaste of the best yet to come.

Implications

If this is the theological model we adapt for our administry, there are at least a few implications. First, how we honor every human being will lead to person-centered behaviors. If every individual is created in the image of God, we default to respecting and valuing each person. None deserves being marginalized. None merits less access to resources. God's good news is for all. God's Spirit is speaking to all in general revelation as a minimum. We treat every individual with mercy and justice. We practice self-giving love in every relationship.

The complement to this person-centeredness is a mission-centeredness. The both/and of the Gospel is to love God and neighbor. That love plays out not only relationally—it also manifests in a relentless press toward God's purposes. The antidote for unhealthy codependence is tenacious mission. While God "wins in the end," we have a role to play in the eschatological flow. We are actors animated by the Holy Spirit and obedient to a heavenly calling. Whether the mission is to martyrdom or to advocacy, to church planting or to chaplaincy, to be a prophetic vanguard or to behind-the-scenes faithfulness, we are on a mission of God.

Third, we can live into what the King James translation calls *longsuffering*.[2] Patience is more than a virtue. It is a discipline. When Isaiah 30:20-21 describes the teacher who will speak the guiding word, one gets a sense of being coached, at times when under duress, as to which way to walk. There may be occasions of waiting at the intersections of life, but we can hold on with anticipation. Even the waiting becomes redemptive as we listen for God's direction. As we walk, we can walk humbly and with confidence that the One who calls is faithful and will ultimately accomplish what God intends.

Fourth, we practice adminstry in an imperfect world being redeemed by God's grace. "Ichabod" has not been written over the world as we know it. In fact, we walk in the full promise that God's kingdom is inbreaking. Christ's birth, life, death, and resurrection have changed everything. All of creation embraces the temporary birth pangs with the expectation that a fallen world will give way to a new heaven and new earth. As God's agents, we do not lose hope. Rather, we seek to embody grace upon grace as we stand against fallenness and incubate faithfulness. God's incarnating presence through us by the Holy Spirit works out both our own salvation and the healing of all creation.

Fifth, that same incarnating presence of the Spirit precedes us into adminstry. The triune God is not limited by our structures and systems, though we believe God can work through them. God's miraculous activity levels the unscalable mountains and smooths the roughest of terrains. We are surrounded with more witnesses than we could imagine who have shown the way. Some of those crowds were once human. Some are angels and archangels. God is at work before we are. Take hope and follow.

Chapter 3
STEWARDING PEOPLE

Organizing Paid and Unpaid Staff

"Called-out ones," those who comprise a local congregation, bear the image of God. Like every human being, they are marked as the prime of God's creation, designed to be in relationship with their Creator. They have been given the gift of free choice and invited to opt for the fullness of life that only the Author of Life can provide. This abundant life described by Jesus often is depicted as a journey, a growing intimacy with God and with one another through Christ.

Missional pastors and leaders embrace this journey as a stewardship of the people entrusted to them. They understand that God's call on any group of individuals is to become a community moving out in faithfulness on purpose. They welcome the rhythms of loving God and one another, living authentically together while engaging others with the hope of Christ. The fruit of their relational life is mission.

The Apostle Paul depicted this existence as a blending of diverse personalities and gifts into a body. Each member of the body has his or her own unique contribution to make. One body part will look and act differently from another. The expertise of the hand will contrast with the role of the eyes. Yet, by design, the members of the body join together in a common life. They have life only as they fully relate to one another. They fulfill a function only as they are animated by the life they share.

Immediately following his discussion of the gifts of the body of Christ in Ephesians 4, Paul gave the bottom line: we are to present every member mature in Christ to the glory of God. Being members of Christ's body is not the end. Serving according to one's giftedness is not the goal. The result God intends is becoming like Christ Jesus. While we are created in the image of God, we are being made into the image of Christ. How we enter into that process, even on a staff team, matters.

Gifted members of the body do not show up fully formed. They may be awkward at first. They may be tired or wounded. They may need some exercise and training. They (and we) require space to grow more into Christlikeness.

I remind my in-laws that I was not responsible for my wife, Yvonne, before I first met her. She had been influenced in her identity by friends and family members long before our paths intersected. She had made her own choices and adapted to the circumstances of her life to that point. Until we came into relationship with one another, who Yvonne had become was the result of biological, emotional, spiritual, and psychological experiences and how she interacted with them.

Once we began our relationship, I could no longer deny the role I play in helping to shape who she is, and is becoming, in Christ. She has her own will; she makes her own decisions. Yet, we now share partial responsibility for the person each of us is becoming. We negotiate behaviors and life direction together. We encounter each day in partnership. When we entered into the marriage covenant, we promised to love each other no matter what might happen. We committed to allow one to help shape the other in self-giving love, however imperfectly.

In the same way, missional pastors and leaders create space for each person within their circle of influence to take the next step in maturity. They steward potent community vibrant with hope and transforming relationships. They view each individual, whether a member of the congregation or an absolute stranger, as one created in the image of God, one being pursued by grace for deeper relationship with the Lord, and as one through whom the mission of God can shine.

18

The Power of Many

Mission is not accomplished alone. From Genesis to Revelation, we see models of community. The seventy nations comprise the inventory of peoples in Genesis 10. Joseph went down to Egypt with an entourage of seventy. Jethro, Moses's Midianite priest/father-in-law, addressed Moses and the elders about how to organize the leaders after their exodus. Seventy elders in Exodus 24 accompanied Moses on Mount Sinai. Ezekiel 8 refers to the seventy elders of Israel. Jesus gathered a dozen men, three of whom comprised the inner circle. He sent seventy (or seventy-two) in Luke 10. One hundred twenty gathered in waiting for Pentecost. Paul constantly referred to ministry companions. The crowds around the throne in Revelation did not arrive there in isolation.

Why is it, then, that we seem to believe in solo ministry performances? Seminaries typically prepare clergy for doing acts of ministry by themselves, whether preaching, counseling, administration, or teaching. We are doing better at embracing the role of laity, but producing individual professionals still seems to be the goal. The dearth of seminary instruction in team dynamics and staffing reflects the assumption that a graduate's first church is likely to be small and have no paid staff, forgetting that unpaid volunteers make great teams as well.

An alternative view, based on the patterns of the biblical narrative, calls for life together scaled for relationship. Whether the leadership pyramid model introduced by Jethro or the temple courts and house-to-house existence of the first church (Acts 2–4), we build associations with sufficient strength and frequency to ensure healthy mission.

From Theology to Practice

If we have a stewardship of leadership, then how do we lay out structures and systems that champion our theology? What practices align with presenting everyone mature in Christ? How do we foster community that calls out the best in unpaid as well as paid "staff"?

Note that I am assuming that everyone in the congregation has a role to play. All baptized Christ-followers are called to ministry. All are talented. All are given at least one gift to offer in the mission of Christ. (This is especially true since spiritual gifts are never for our own enjoyment alone. They are invested in the larger community through us.) Whether or not we are paid by the local church to do so, we all have ministry to do.

The challenges come when we treat paid staff like volunteers and volunteers like hirelings. Many congregations avoid institutional terms entirely. If every person bears the imago Dei, then we are an assortment of holy and cherished individuals. No hirelings here. If our role is determined by the call and gifting of God, then the lines between paid and unpaid blur. We all have responsibilities and relationships on a shared mission. If we are joint heirs with Christ of the mystery of God, then we share an eternal trust. If we are to provoke one another to full maturity (Heb 10:24-25), then we all have entered a formational community.

What form the staffing structure takes will depend in part on the polity of the organization. How are decisions made? Who needs to be in the discernment process? How are people and resources mobilized for mission? If we are United Methodist, how many boards and committees are required? (One group of superintendents and their bishop boiled it down for a church of only nine members—three for staff parish, three for trustees, and three for finance. In aggregate, these nine double as the Administrative Council and a subset of them serve as the Lay Leadership Committee. Even then, not every trustee must be a member of the church, so fewer than nine might be possible, though not necessarily prudent.)

Within the polity framework, there are particular functions to consider. How shall we worship, and who will serve that element of our life together? How shall we care for one another, and who will provide the safety nets of compassion? How shall we do disciple building, and who will lead that effort? What administry is needed, and who will orchestrate that function?

In an established church, the current functions may or may not be optimal. How will we continually assess the effectiveness of our life together with an eye to our "ongoing conversion"?[1] To borrow Bishop Bruce Ough's categories, as popularized by Bishop Robert Schnase, how shall we provide for radical hospitality, passionate worship, intentional faith development, risk-taking mission and service, and extravagant generosity? Who will take the lead for each one of these values?[2]

Mobilizing Gifts for Fruitful Ministry

A recent study by McKinsey and Company explored the ways high-performing organizations leverage the talents of their researchers. They discovered four behaviors common among the best practices. They recruited diverse team members for their potential, intentionally developed them, and rewarded their success. Sounds pretty basic, yes?[3] Notice how they executed these behaviors. Team members were recruited for their prior experience, how well they fit the culture of the organization, and their intrinsic qualities, such as adaptability. Once selected, the team members were involved in a structured mentoring process, often in the form of apprenticeship, with an annual personal development plan. They understood the consequences of poor performance, their achievements were celebrated, and there were rewards for effectively fulfilling their role.

Seen through the lens of scripture, these behaviors are transferrable to the church and parachurch. To be a disciple is to be an apprentice, to adopt the lifestyle and qualities of the one to whom one is apprenticing. Compare vocational practices over the centuries. Employers selected protégés carefully. Early in the tradition, the craft would pass from parent to child. As others also learned the trade, employers could become more selective to ensure innate potential for the vocation. Our apprenticeship to Jesus, our first calling, can unfold in every relationship. Then, as one apprehends and is apprehended by the faith, one can test the Spirit on the particular giftings entrusted to the new disciple. While the novice may not have exercised a particular ministry before, there are signposts along the way that indicate a propensity for areas of service. Holy experiments conducted with a trusted mentor confirm how one is equipped for ministry. All the while, going further in discipleship ripens the fruit of the Spirit in the individual, enriching the intrinsic qualities of faithfulness. Reflective engagement uncovers next steps toward Christlikeness. The body of Christ's ministry into the world makes clear the stakes for apprenticeship in community: people hungry for divine hope. As one member of the body rejoices, all rejoice. When one weeps, all weep. The joy of fruitful obedience incentivizes continuing growth in the individual and in the body.

First Call: To Christ	Vocation in the Church	Vocation beyond Church
Grow in Love: God	Worship with Your Life	Overflow Love
Grow in Love: Neighbor	Live in Community	Live Authentically
Practice the Means of Grace	Demonstrate Faithfulness	Lay Down Your Life
Discover Gift(s) & Vocation	Serve Contagiously	Work as a Minister
Apprentice Others	Release Others	"Salt the Oats"

Figure 3.1: A Vocational Matrix

One developmental heuristic to consider, as shown above, is to think through the three callings of a believer: to Christ, to vocation, and to location.[4] Our first relationship is to be with God through Jesus Christ by the power of the Holy Spirit. The Gospels remind us that loving God is mirrored as we love our neighbors. John Wesley captured the historic practices that position the believer for the Spirit's presence. In the worshipping community we begin to see how God has gifted us and where God might maximize who God created us to be. Just as we have been discipled into biblical fidelity, we then invest in the lives of others on the faith journey.

Covenant life within the local congregation (paid or unpaid) entails a similar flow. Loving God with others, especially as expressed in corporate worship, centers individuals and the whole. Transparent community like that of Acts 2 and Acts 4 sharpens us. Living grace-full in worship and community catalyzes faithfulness in oneself and others. As we offer our giftedness, the Spirit animates the entire group with the beauty of the body working together. Brothers and sisters gain courage and stamina as they live into their own vocations.

Loving God and others beyond the church (paid or unpaid) winsomely points to our Creator. Our vulnerability grants permission for others to "taste and see" that the Lord is good (see Psalm 34:8 NRSV).

Our sacramental living becomes the vehicle of grace to those around us. Our sensitivity to what God is doing in those with whom we relate gives us eyes to see where we can salt conversations and experiences with the gospel as Christ's ambassadors.

Staffing Systems in a Christian Organization

Since a primary goal of "called-out ones" is each person maturing in Christ, staffing systems in a Christian organization serve to ensure the health and growth of individuals while fulfilling the mission of the organization. State and federal laws provide an added context within which we function, so staffing systems must accommodate legal as well as theological principles. While there may be a few exceptions for religious organizations in state and federal statutes, most legal regulations apply to all groups and institutions, regardless of the religious status. The remaining sections of this chapter will incorporate ethical and legal considerations into our discussion.

Most congregations in North America have at least a part-time pastor committed to preach at the main worship service; perform ceremonial functions, such as baptisms, weddings, and funerals; and serve as primary caregiver to the members. The larger the church, the likelier it is that the pastor is full-time; that is, that the church's salary is the pastor's primary source of income. Also, how involved the pastor is in the governance of the church is strongly correlated to the size of the congregation. Lyle Schaller, in his book *The Seven-Day-a-Week Church,* suggests that the larger the church, the more central to decision making the pastor becomes.[5] The larger the church, the higher the probability that the congregation has added staff to help support the ministries of the church. Often the first paid staff member to be added after the pastor is a part-time secretary or youth director. Immediately the pastor is expected to have some ability to lead a multi-staff church in collaboration with the church's personnel committee. Most denominations or associations address the role and expectations of the pastor in their polity, but do not provide much formal direction for other church staff. How should a congregation think about staffing for mission?

Staffing the "Volunteer Organization"

Pastors often cross into full-time employment as the congregation grows beyond a hundred attenders or so in size. Many regions of the United States often use the rule of thumb of 150 in attendance to be able to afford a full-time, fully credentialed clergy person. Pastoral salary packages can be expensive. The average package for a pastor in the United States, including housing, insurance, and other standard benefits, was $90,643 in 2016.[6] At some point in a congregation's growth, the benefit of a full-time pastor outweighs the cost savings of staying small.

Each parish will need to evaluate two questions: (1) At what points in our growth will we add paid staff to our team? And (2) How will we continue to develop our (paid and unpaid) staff to ensure a healthy congregation? The danger is to consider the pastor the "hired gun" who performs all of the ministry while the members and constituents watch from the sidelines. The ideal is positioning the pastor and other staff as equippers of the congregation, ones who identify gifts and mobilize individuals for effective ministry. Only in North America have I witnessed the temptation to buy enough professionals to do the ministry of the church. In other regions of the world, unpaid servants accomplish the mission as part of their normal journey in faith. I once asked a pastor from Kenya who was serving a church in the United States to describe which church was easier to lead. "Oh," he said, "the Kenyan church was much easier because, in my country, people did the ministry. Here, people think the pastor should do the ministry."

When considering what salary to provide for a new position, seek comparable salary rates from area schools and churches. There are usually good staff salary studies done by denominations and area chambers of commerce. Another option is to buy reports from national associations such as Christianity Today/Church Law Today (http://store.churchlaw todaystore.com/20cohaforchs.html) and The Church Network (http://www.ministrypay.com). The data can be sorted by region and position, as well as by church attendance and budget size.

Paid staff rightly expect a role description that outlines performance expectations. (Unpaid staff would be wise to ask for the same courtesy.)

Legally, the organization will need to classify whether this position is an exempt or non-exempt employee. Exempt employees typically oversee staff and/or major areas of the organization. Non-exempt, or hourly, employees have a more limited scope of responsibility. Be aware that new standards for determining whether a person is exempt or non-exempt were scheduled to take effect in 2016 and are, at this writing, being appealed in the courts. One of the criteria for making that exempt vs. non-exempt determination is salary range. An employment attorney, human resources executive, or appropriate denominational staff can help interpret the current Department of Labor standards.

Once the decision for adding staff is made, assuming the need has been clearly defined, resources for the position have been allocated and a role description written, the hiring process moves to conducting the search. Many congregations approach a new staff position as a way to enlarge ministry by hiring an inexperienced person whom the pastor can mentor into the role. No evidence of prior understanding or practice necessary. While that may be a very viable strategy, I encourage churches to avoid that option solely to save money. In larger churches particularly, there is less time to mentor staff into the expertise required. The insights a veteran can bring to a new staff team might provide fresh perspectives and breakthrough learnings.

Building a deep pool of applicants necessitates creative networking. Typically, denominational sources must be combined with alternatives, such as www.churchstaffing.com, university and seminary alumni offices, and possibly the use of Christian staff search consultants. The larger the church, the longer a search takes, even if the plan is to raise up (home grow) the new staff member from within the church. One ideal is to identify at least five to ten viable applicants for any search. Twenty would be better.

Once the pool of applicants has been gathered, the résumés and cover letters reviewed, applicant references checked, and a few (a minimum of two) candidates selected for interviews, phone and then face-to-face conversations will help the interview team narrow the selection. Avoid one-on-one interviews, since they can lead to miscommunication. Two or three interviewers with the candidate makes for a richer interchange. Ask the same general questions of each applicant, and be sure to follow federal guidelines on what questions may or may not be asked. Probe for transferrable experiences, demonstrable expertise (by asking, "What have you done?" rather than "What might you do?"), and strong fit with the current staff culture. Good chemistry with the staff team matters as much as competence and character. Interview for the best match to the role description, taking care to surface any unspoken expectations and behaviors that exist in any organization. How strong in the faith an applicant needs to be depends on how near the heart of the ministry the potential staff member will serve. Billy Graham has talked about hiring nonbelievers for some non-central positions as a form of witness. Never soft-sell the need for high commitment to the organization's mission.

The Interview Process

Title VII of the Civil Rights Act of 1964, along with other federal guidelines (see http://www.eeoc.gov/facts/qanda.html), applies to religious institutions as well. These regulations prohibit discrimination in hiring, firing, promotion, transfer, compensation, and admission to training programs due to race, color, religion, sex, age, disability, veterans status, marital status, pregnancy, genetic information, or national origin. Churches can have some leniency around faith issues, but often less than many congregations want to assume. Unless doing so would create an undue hardship, all employers are expected to accommodate the religious beliefs of staff and potential staff. In biblical terms, we are expected to be hospitable and just with all people.

Violating the federal guidelines can have serious consequences for Christian organizations. They could lose their nonprofit status and/or be sued by an employee or potential employee. If the violation excludes more protected classes of people (e.g., race or marital status) than a nonprotected class, then the organization is liable for state and federal penalties. It is not appropriate, for example, to ask an applicant's age. For help in knowing what to ask in an interview, suggested interview questions are provided in the appendix.

Once a new staff member is selected, an offer of salary package and staff benefits, a staff policy handbook, and a start date are presented for consideration. If the offer is made in a formal letter, often acceptance of the offer is indicated by the applicant's signature at the bottom of the letter. (Be careful, in drafting the letter, not to guarantee an annualized amount since this can be construed as a promise whether or not the staff person stays employed. An attorney or human resources executive can help craft the language.) Be sure to indicate how the church will help orient the new staff member to the role. A training period may important. A cordial beginning sets the tone for fruitful, long-term relationships.

Calling Out God's Best in One Another

Mission always elicits the best from those who join the adventure. When witnessed in community, there is an air of expectancy, a compelling sense of waiting on tiptoe. That attitude of anticipation calls out God's best in each participant. The barriers to missional effectiveness command superhuman capacity to hurdle them. Unless the Spirit works miracles through frail human beings, the mission will never be accomplished.

Stewarding paid and unpaid staff in a missional organization entails clearly stating current expectations based on seen and unseen criteria. How do we attend to the eternal quality of our work together while adapting the best practices of staff development? How does everyone on the team have confidence in the direction of the team and the anticipated fruit (i.e., results) of faithful ministry? When a team member is failing to bear fruit according to the member's potential and the ministry needs, what happens next? What federal regulations impact how a church or parachurch organization operates?

A common adage states, "The best time to fire a staff member is before the member gets hired." A thorough hiring process will be the first step toward long-term staff relationships. The second contribution to long tenure is an intentional staff development process that includes regular assessment, tapping into individual and corporate dreams and occasional holy experiments.

While many congregations conduct annual reviews of staff member performance, a minimum of biannual check-ins communicates an appreciation of the pace of change in any person and his or her family. A lot can shift in six months. It also acknowledges that ministry constantly evolves, whether we notice it or not. Formal conversations twice a year with a culture of biweekly or monthly calibration discussions ensures that everyone stays on the same page. A sample guide for a midyear (less formal) check-in as well as an annual staff review are provided at the end of this chapter. The more frequent discussions address ministry projects, people development, and use of resources as the staff person helps to align all activity with the mission. The staff review creates space for prayer and discernment as the staff member and team leader engage in the practice of biblical oversight as good shepherds of the flock.

The biannual conversations and monthly discussions are far more than managerial. They serve aspirational purposes, allowing the staff member and team leader to tap dreams and visions. One of the saddest reports I receive from departing staff is "They never asked me about my hopes and dreams. They never listened to what possibilities I saw in the congregation." Mission always sparks dreams. Spirit-animated organizations embrace future horizons of opportunity, more than any one person can accomplish and greater than any one individual's perspective. If ministry activities are about God's mystery, dreaming is unavoidable. Monthly and biannual check-ins center on what is and what might be, should the Lord open the doors.

A natural question that emerges from aspirational discernment is "Now what?" As prayer-guided dreams, gifted people, and breathtaking mission interact in a kind of divine alchemy, ideas for worthy experiments rise to the surface. Where might the Spirit be doing a new thing? Do we have eyes to see it? Will we exercise faith to test missional possibilities in holy pilot projects? Since the biblical principle is "no risk, no miracle," how might the staff team step into the water to witness how the sea might become dry land? Moses likely learned to trust God in the decades as a herdsman for Jethro in preparation for leading God's people out of Egypt. He grew in wise leadership. Every pilot project affords moments of learning as the congregation takes the next step toward God's dream. Seemingly small acts of faithfulness become the foundation for God's great movements.

Regardless of the agenda for the biannual and monthly discussions, document the conversations to track growth. This could take the form of a journal or blog, but allow the spiritual discipline of writing to be another avenue for the Spirit to speak into the staff team. Review the writings at least semiannually to learn where growth is happening and how new direction is unfolding. How well have resources been stewarded for mission? Where is the staff member best investing in the ministry? Where might some holy pilot projects merit greater attention or be developing into a major addition to our work together? What is the Spirit trying to teach us?

In the (hopefully) rare scenarios where gaps in staff performance begin to be recognized, the individual growth plan that accompanies the annual review takes on a different meaning. The monthly calibration discussions usually catch diversions from the mission before they become serious. Like the autopilot on an international flight, the corrections to trajectory are made en route. Systems issues, which often are the culprit in performance gaps, are addressed along the way, and behaviors can be altered. Invitations for behavior change start with coaching by the team leader and occur "off the record." If the inappropriate behavior continues, then a verbal warning is given and documented in the personnel file. The next level of correction is a written warning, which might be followed by a probationary period and/or suspension. The final option is termination.

Never remove notations from staff files. Instead, document the changes in behavior with a new note, indicating what issue the new note addresses and how the behavior has changed, along with what remaining expectations might still be in place.

Whether in correcting detrimental behavior or enforcing positive behavior, keep record of investments made in learning and the actions that have been observed. If the staff member has acted well, document it. If the staff member still has gaps in performance, document it. Journaling the growth, along with measurable instructions on how to improve, will typically bear the desired results. Match the seriousness of the intervention with the seriousness of the behavior. Remember that each member of the team, irrespective of performance, bears the image of God and has particular gifts for ministry, whether or not the ideal context for that ministry is the current time and place. Seek solutions without blame or shame. Redeem the inherent conflict as imperfect human beings seeking the best for one another. Should the fit between the congregation and the staff member become incompatible, explore avenues for repositioning the staff member in another place of ministry as appropriate.

Many regions in the United States have "at will" employment laws. There does not need to be a particular reason for separating an employee from the employer. As long as no legally discriminatory action accompanies the termination, the employer can dismiss a person "at will." Some states have many more regulations governing employment that will apply to religious institutions. When considering the termination of a staff member, it is wise to consult a trusted employment attorney to ensure compliance with legal guidelines.

In Christian organizations it can be tempting to raise concerns about attitude issues in the staff member. Attitude is not admissible evidence in employment matters. Only documentable performance behavior can be addressed. (There may be a case to be made in the courts regarding divergent religious beliefs, but that would be a difficult argument once the staff member joins the payroll.) Always focus on actions, not attitudes, whether in correcting or renforcing behavior.

One other note: A staff member has the right to respond to disciplinary action. It is one of the reasons both the team leader and the staff member sign annual reviews and individual growth plans. Invite responses, both verbally and in writing, to offer every opening for improvement. The staff member and the team leader are not required to agree with each other's perspective and might even state the disagreement in writing. Nonetheless, the employment relationship is dialogical, not dictatorial.

Learning and Celebrating Together

One of my favorite memories from a church where I served was the annual church conference. Most pastors will recoil at the idea of actually enjoying the annual meeting, but our staff had reengineered what had often been a boring business meeting into a high celebration of faithfulness in the congregation. We still held the necessary votes for new leaders and staff salaries, but those items were limited to ten minutes or so in the agenda. The bulk of our energy was focused on a "This Is Your Life" experience in a pleasant dinner setting. Ministry area leaders were invited to identify one individual in their area who exemplified the mission and values of the congregation. That person was then nominated for a servant leadership award that became highly coveted because only those who excelled at loving Christ and serving others qualified for consideration.

The pastor opened the evening with an inspiring reminder of our covenant as coworkers in the kingdom of God, dependent on the Holy Spirit and one another for the ministry God had given us. Then, one by one, ministry area leaders would come to the microphone to first describe, and then name, the recipient of the annual award for their area. As the description was read, the audience would begin to quietly guess at who was about to be honored. They would look around the room, trying to identify the person being named. Often that recipient's eyes would begin to well up as he realized that he was the one to receive the award. Once the ministry area leader announced the name, the crowd would join in wonderful applause and thanksgiving for the nominee. The annual celebrations of God's graciousness through those honored stoked the faith of everyone in the room.

It is no accident that a portion of the tithe designated in the early Israelite worship, and passed down to us, includes the party. God knows we need to celebrate. We are designed to revel in the goodness of our creating and sustaining Lord. As the people of God, we mark God's character with worship and thanksgiving, honoring the One who redeems us and allows us to participate in eternal purpose. In the same way, we are called to applaud the goodness of God when it shows up through God's people.

How will the congregation "provoke one another to love and good deeds" according to Hebrews 10:24 (NRSV)? Where will there be occasions for encouraging one another in faithfulness? How will the people be able to watch and see the hand of God at work around the faith community? Create openings for honoring committed paid and unpaid staff who embrace the call of God. In public and private ways, build up the saints for the work of the ministry. Slow down enough to bask in the wonders of the Spirit's handiwork, thereby planting seeds of hope and confidence in God's future.

In addition, host learning moments that equip staff members for increased effectiveness. Learn from neighboring congregations who might be one step ahead in a particular area of ministry. We would often do staff field trips to learn from staff teams around us. Budget for strategic conferences and events that motivate staff teams toward new practices and remind them about their role in God's promise. Debrief internal ministry experiences regularly so the staff team becomes expert as a learning community. Engage consultants as appropriate to bring outside perspectives to the staff team. Establish a reading habit, individually and corporately, that stirs up ideas for growth. An organization that ceases to celebrate and learn atrophies. In time, it becomes hollow.

Conflict: Speaking Truth in Love

All of this watching and provoking in community naturally produces friction. There may be seasons when an individual or group would rather not take the next step in effectiveness. Calling the best out of one another can feel like badgering if not done well. Personalities clash. Styles contrast. Speaking the truth to one another might occasionally come seasoned with too negligible a measure of love. Minor irritations can escalate into full-blown confrontations.

Conflict is good—at least that is what the scholars say. In fact, the absence of conflict often indicates the void of commitment and trust. But how do staff teams foster appropriate conflict? How do we live between avoidance and apoplexy?

Healthy conflict operates best in an atmosphere of trust. Trust generates from relationship. As one author asks, "Will you love me enough to trust me?"[7] We may initially trust a person's title or position, but lasting trust builds as we experience trustworthiness through relationship.

A colleague and I recently worked with a church team where the pastor spent minimal time with the staff. They appreciated his sermons, his sense of humor, and his reputation as an excellent caregiver. Yet, they did not know him well enough to know if they could trust him with more than the weekly check-in, where everyone reported what they were working on. They wanted to believe in him. He realized he needed to give them more access to who he was, his authenticty, so they likewise would be more authentic with him. Until they could better predict how he would behave with the tough items, they were unwilling to risk conflict.

Susan Scott, in her book *Fierce Conversations,* invites teams into healthy, vibrant communication that does not ignore the natural challenges to full disclosure. By that, she does not mean airing dirty laundry. She does intend courageous honesty that no longer avoids sensitive issues. Listening plays a critical role. So do humility and objectivity. As groups establish cultures of trust and wade into the deeper waters of transparency, satisfaction and effectiveness rise.[8]

The basic conflict management styles include competition ("I win, you lose"), avoidance, accommodation ("you win, I lose"), compromise, and collaboration (problem solving). Research tells us we each have a default or preferred style. Pepper that style with personalities and temperaments, and the drama can get interesting. Knowing one's style provides the first step toward better conflict engagement. Understanding the best contexts for each style creates a behavioral menu when conflict arises. For example, if the room is on fire, collaboration might be more useful than avoidance. No one style is ideal for every situation. The emotions that accompany our style approach can make the experience more meaningful, positively and negatively.

One of the best rubrics for participating in conflict is Scott's confrontation model. In chapter 4 she invokes a conflict-as-learning opportunity approach that states the conflict in the first sixty seconds of the discussion. In that first minute, the initiator identifies the issue, gives an illustration, names the emotions around the issue, clarifies what is at stake in the issue, confesses his or her contribution to the issue and the hope to resolve it, and then invites the other person to respond. The ensuing exchange involves listening deeply and probing for meanings so the person knows you understand his or her position. The final steps include moving toward accountable resolution of the issue.

Few conflicts are pleasant. Healthy resolution requires practice bathed in trust and forgiveness. The tensions do not magically disappear, but they can enrich the relational soil of fruit-bearing ministry.

Summary

A church or parachurch ministry exists to reveal the glory of God on the earth. As "called-out ones," we gather paid and unpaid people together to worship and serve according to God's purpose. How we identify, enlist, develop, and deploy these staff members will bear witness to the God we proclaim. Our biblical frameworks for mobilizing the saints for ministry include the contextual realities of legal and ethical expectations. Our role is to ensure healthy and clear expectations for doing ministry together that move us forward in God's dream for our world.[9]

First Church Role Description

Role: Administrative Assistant
Accountable to: Pastor
FLSA Classification: Non-Exempt
Date: January 5, 2016

Purpose: To support the pastor and other key leaders of the church in mobilizing the resources of the congregation for ministry. This includes project management, mobilizing unpaid staff, and creating administrative systems and processes.

Desired Gifts and Abilities: This person will likely have helping and administrative gifts. S/he will have exceptional organizational ability and will be experienced in complex project management with proven skills in mobilizing people. S/he will demonstrate high-level communication and problem-solving strengths as well as an impressive facility with office technology.

Apprenticed to: No one at this time
Apprenticing: Selected nonpaid staff

Contribution to Shared Mission:

1. Provide project level support for the pastor.
2. Enlist and equip nonpaid staff for reception, office, and secretarial support for the pastor and ministries of the church.
3. Ensure effective administrative systems and processes for the church's ministries, including calendaring, financial accounting, document creation, graphic production, facilities and insurance records, recruiting volunteers, and project management.

Church Resources Available to You:

1. Semiprivate work area with desk, phone, computer, soft-ware, office equipment, and so on.

2. $50/month reimbursement for church-related cell phone usage.

3. Two weeks of vacation annually plus paid holidays per the staff handbook.

First Church Team Member Check-In

Date:

1. How has your understanding of our mission changed since our last check-in?

2. Where do you see gaps between what we espouse and how we act?

3. Where are we best utilizing your gifts and strengths?

4. How might we better position you for your optimal contribution to our shared mission?

5. What resources do you need to live out your role with us?

6. What do we need to do differently to make your contribution easier?

7. What else do we need to make sure we talk about?

First Church Staff Review

___ Paid Staff   ___ Unpaid Staff

___ Annual Review   ___ New Staff Review

___ Other Review: _____

Staff Member:

Role:

Reviewer:

Date:

In the following narratives, please indicate whether the staff member excels, is satisfactory, or needs to improve in each of the areas.

Stated expectations from Role Description and Individual Growth Plan that are relevant for this review:

1. _____

2. _____

3. _____

4. _____

5. _____

Quality of Contributions to Our Shared Mission

1. Understanding one's role and contribution to the church's mission: How well does this staff member excel in effectively fulfilling the mission given the expectations above? Is this staff member growing in the role?

2. Ability to analyze and problem solve: How well does this staff member demonstrate thorough and timely identification of, and initial solutions for, areas of concern in our shared

mission? How does the staff member engage others in the decision-making process as appropriate?

3. Integrative service: How well does this staff member exhibit personal organization, initiative, and efficiency in accomplishing the mission? How well does the staff member leverage ideas, people, time, and resources to creatively fulfill the expectations above?

4. Healthy relationships: How well does this staff member interact with peers, supervisors, and those whom the member mobilizes? How well does the staff member value, communicate, direct, receive feedback, motivate, and help grow people?

5. Other areas for review given the expectations above:

Staff member response to this review:

Reviewer response to this review:

Follow-up steps (e.g., updating role description or personal growth plan):
1. _____
2. _____
3. _____

Staff member signature and date:

Reviewer signature and date:

Sample Interview Questions

1. What attracted you to this position?

2. How would you summarize the job expectations for this role? What relational and technical expertise will be needed to succeed in it?

3. What of your past experiences prepare you well to fulfill this role?

4. What is your vision for this role? What might it become in the next three to five years?

5. Where might you need to grow into the job description? Where might you be overqualified?

6. Describe the quality of relationship you seek to establish with co-workers.

7. How would a supervisor best position you for effectiveness?

8. What is your conflict management style? How do you help redeem the conflicts that naturally arise in the workplace?

9. How do you develop other people? How do you manage projects? Which of the two functions are more energizing for you?

10. What else do you wish we would have asked you during this interview?

First Church Individual Growth Plan

___ Paid Staff   ___ Unpaid Staff
___ Annual Growth Plan   ___ New Staff Growth Plan
___ Other: _____

Staff Member:
Role:
Reviewer:
Date:

Overall Contribution to Shared Mission
1. Specific action(s) to be taken:

2. Resources required:

3. Time frame to accomplish these actions:

4. Measurable evidence of growth:

Specific Projects
1. Specific action(s) to be taken:

2. Resources required:

3. Time frame to accomplish these actions:

4. Measurable evidence of growth:

Relationships with Others

1. Specific action(s) to be taken:

2. Resources required:

3. Time frame to accomplish these actions:

4. Measurable evidence of growth:

Staff member signature and date:

Team leader signature and date:

Chapter 4
STEWARDING RELATIONSHIPS

The Power of Networks

Psychologists suggest that an emotionally healthy person does not have the capacity for large numbers of intimate friendships. Most of us have fewer than ten or twelve individuals who are our closest friends. Our relational bandwidth determines what types of relationships we have and how many people fall into each category.

Social anthropologist Edward T. Hall coined the term *proxemics* in the 1960s to describe how humans negotiate spatial relationships. Public spaces require very little connection apart from a common cause, such as loyalty to a local sports team. Social spaces are those neighborly relationships where we can determine whether or not to go deeper in our vulnerability. Personal spaces are those close friends with whom we can keep confidences and foster one-on-one relationships. Intimate spaces are those surroundings where each knows the naked truth about the other without shame or guilt.[1]

Joseph Myers uses Hall's model to critique the "one size fits all" approach to small groups of the local congregation. He suggests in his book *The Search to Belong: Rethinking Intimacy, Community and Small Groups* that we present ourselves in different ways in each of these four spaces.

There can be significant spiritual growth in any one of the four surroundings. While the spatial competencies are different for each setting, all four are relevant for our social well-being.[2]

It is healthy to appropriately present different personas in different settings. One would not expect a high degree of vulnerability in a public space, for example. At the same time, particularly in an era that values authenticity, people do seek relationships that are attractional within the boundaries of each type of space. It does not take long to discover when a person is "wearing a mask" in inappropriate ways.

In spiritual terms, there is another type of spatial relationship: one's relationship with oneself and one's Creator. This secret space can be one of hidden agendas and significant pain. The fewer secrets we have, the less likely that we will be tied down by fear, guilt, and shame. God invites us to the unfolding work of grace and healing so we no longer need to hide any facet of our being. Stepping into the light with our relationship with God releases us to do the same, as congruent, with the other spatial relationships in community.

Probably in a time of his greatest weakness, the prophet Elijah imagined himself as the lone voice for God. He had just witnessed Yahweh's victory over the prophets of Baal (1 Kings 18). Suddenly he found himself in isolation and begging for God to kill him. One of the Lord's instructions to Elijah was a word of hope: that God had preserved seven thousand Israelites who had not bent their knee to Baal (1 Kings 19). In his depression he had forgotten God's great power and provision.

No surprise that one of the hallmarks of the post-Pentecost (Acts 2) church was the quality of their love for one another in Christian community. In spite of the famous stories of spiritual hermitage during the Middle Ages where desert mothers and fathers would spent extended time in isolation, God's first design is to raise up "communities of prophets," like those who accompanied Elijah and Elisha, who serve as God's divine network of relationships. In twenty-first-century terms, God has established billions of Christ-followers clustered in churches, parachurch organizations, and other faith-based gatherings to witness to God's goodness around the world. We are never alone. In fact, we miss the richness and

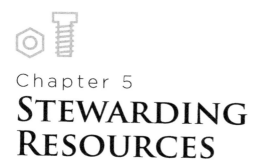

Chapter 5
STEWARDING RESOURCES

Finances and Budgeting

While the Lord owns "the cattle on a thousand hills" (Psalm 50:10), those "cattle" require good herd management in an age where dollars, rather than cattle, are now the normal currency for a congregation. All of God's resources are available to God's people. The challenge, once those resources amass, is to steward them well. Most church leaders are unschooled in financial management. Seminaries and divinity schools teach the classical package of homiletics, counseling, worship, Bible, theology, and church history. Few pastoral leaders are introduced to basic fiscal practices, such as budgeting and fiduciary responsibilities. This chapter will serve as an overview of critical financial management principles.

Not-for-profit financial management differs from most corporate practices in the nomenclature and what qualifies as value. For-profit entities pay attention to profits and losses (P&L) as a key measure of assets. Not-for-profit entities (NPOs) count income and outgo as well, but use the terms *revenues* and *expenditures*.

For church and parachurch organizations, income primarily comes in the form of contributions. These revenues are used to support the staff and services provided for the beneficiaries of the organization. There are assets and liabilities, budgets and balances, audits and accountability, all for the purpose of accomplishing the organization's mission with fiscal integrity. The official guide on financial management in the United States is the Financial Accounting Standards Board (FASB). It "maintains the *FASB Accounting Standards Codification*™ (Accounting Standards Codification) which represents the source of authoritative standards of accounting and reporting, other than those issued by the SEC [Securities Exchange Commission], recognized by the FASB to be applied by nongovernmental entities."[1] In other words, there are commonly accepted financial guidelines that direct how not-for-profit organizations, such as churches and parachurches, care for their financial assets.

From Worship to Offering Counters

A later chapter will address a theology of giving. For the purposes of this chapter, we are reminded that God creates all that is good and shares a portion of God's good provision with us. We are invited to demonstrate our gratitude for God's care via living in a spirit of generosity. Appreciative hearts overflow. In terms of tangible resources, we demonstrate our thankfulness with tithes and offerings, usually through the vehicle of the local church. We will use the term *donor* for those who give those tithes and offerings since it is frequently how the FASB describes one who makes a contribution to an entity.

The ushers walk the aisle in nearly predictable fashion in most congregations. Some may wear white gloves. Some might use metal offering plates instead of cloth bags with fancy handles. Some congregations might take multiple offerings in a single worship service. Other congregations might put offering boxes near the sanctuary door. The purpose is the same: to gather the tithes and offerings from attenders to support the ministries of the church. The cash and checks are secured after the worship service and later counted, the amounts and corresponding donor names recorded in some form, and the monies deposited in the bank for the church leadership to administer. Donors trust the church to have reasonable safeguards for how the monies are tracked from the moment they are entrusted to the ushers until the cash is distributed in mission.

The higher the trust, communicated by well-established standards of accountability, the less reluctant the donor base is to be generous. They see the facilities and programming around them. They hear sermons and teachings on God's benchmarks for giving. They warm to the mission of a local congregation dedicated to making Christ known. They understand the liabilities inherent in salaries, utility bills, and outreach. They may read the weekly financial and attendance reports found in many church bulletins. They want to believe that the church they love treats their gifts as "blood money," a sacred and sacrificial share in the life of God on earth.

As the offerings are carried out of the worship space, they are either taken to an office for two or more unrelated (not from the same family) offering counters to process them or, better, placed in a safe for the counters to process later that day or the next. I recommend not leaving the weekly offering on the church premises overnight. The better practice is to have two people transfer the gifts from the church to the night depository of the bank, where the counters can pick it up when they are ready to do their work. The Offering Tracking Log (below) serves as an example of how to record the money transfers.

Most churches use some type of administrative software for recording donations and processing payables.[2] No congregation should be doing this work with pen and paper in the twenty-first century. The Internal Revenue Service expects that every church and parachurch has established reliable and thorough accounting systems to meet reporting requirements. For example, every not-for-profit, including churches, is expected to file a Form 990 annually. Every donor is required to have documentation of their charitable contributions from the recipient of those gifts. Every church financial audit will want clear paper trails that track the monies from the moment it lands in the offering plate until it is expended for organizational mission-related activities.

As the offering counters sit down to tally the weekend giving, two or more nonrelated individuals are segregating cash from checks and ensuring the amounts are credited to the appropriate constituent. There may be some who give electronically whose generosity will also need to be recorded. There are likely monies from Sunday school classes, small groups, and major church events. All income typically funnels through this weekly crew of faithful stewards, who then certify that each dollar lands in its proper repository. In doing so, contributions records are updated for each donor and church leaders are encouraged by replenished revenues with which to serve the mission. After the collections are counted and posted, the donations are taken to the bank for deposit, reports are given to the church secretary for filing, and the counting team rests for another week. A sample tracking log for money transfers follows.

Offering Tracking Log

Offering to Safe	Safe to Bank	Bank to Counters	Counters to Bank
Sarah Jones	Jack Christoff	Estelle Jackson	Estelle Jackson
Jennifer Awali	Sam Mason	Sherry Smith	Sherry Smith
9/23/12 10:14 a.m.	9/23/12 12:10 p.m.	9/24/12 9:05 a.m.	9/24/12 11:35 a.m.

Each time money is transferred from one location to another, two signatures are required. This will typically satisfy insurance expectations and document good fiduciary practices.

Also, a quick additional word on electronic giving. Many households in a congregation are accustomed to paying bills online through their bank. Some may opt to set up their charitable giving as a recurring "bill" to be paid through the banking institution. This ensures greater reliability in donations and allows the donor to avoid the costs of checks and, possibly, postage. Many congregations make online giving easier by using electronic donation services like easytithe.com and simplegive.com. There is an administrative fee for these services, but the benefits of increased regular income offset the costs. You can research these services online and through sites like nacba.net and ecfa.org. We will discuss the theological and worship rubric considerations in an ensuing chapter. For now, be aware that the electronic giving trend is growing, and each congregation will want to provide opportunities for those wanting to utilize online processing to express their generosity.

Creating the Budget

Nearly every organization operates on a budget. While there are multiple paths to putting the numbers together in a budgeting process, the cleanest is to use a zero-based strategy that begins with the strategic plan and mission of the organization. Why do we exist? For churches, what is our particular call to serve our community? What will be our priorities for the ensuing year? Those priorities dictate what gets the most attention in the budgeting process.

Every organization will have certain fixed costs, such as salaries and utilities, that will need to be accommodated. People are the engine of any enterprise, and some of them need to be paid. Churches need pastors and may be large enough to require staff. If so, there are likely facility costs for housing the ministry.

The challenge comes when the fixed costs consume too large a percentage of the income. For example, if personnel costs (salaries plus benefits plus taxes) exceed 60 percent of the income, then most churches are on the edge of decline. After paying for utilities and the remaining fixed costs, little income will remain for programs and ministries. If, on the other hand, personnel costs are closer to 40 percent of the budget, then it is likely the church has abundant cash flow for creative outreach.

The temptation will be to build next year's spending plan by adding 2 or 3 percent to this year's budget line items. Unfortunately, that incremental approach fails to assess emerging needs. It assumes programs or ministries continue to be vital forever and the community being served never changes. In fact, as the context shifts, with new people entering and others leaving, ministry opportunities change. What worked last year may not work next year. The programs we initiated two years ago may have met their intended goals. As always, the Spirit may be doing a new thing and requires us to reallocate our resources to go where the Spirit is blowing.

The critical budgeting question is, given where the Spirit has called us and is leading us, how shall we invest our assets in ministry next year? The question is not necessarily, What can we afford? Nor is it, What do we want to do? Rather, through careful prayer and discernment, determine what God is asking of the congregation over the next twelve to eighteen months. If the strategic plan is mature enough, how do the priorities of the next year move us toward our vision and mission five years from now?

The budget is too important to negotiate among a closed group—for example, the finance committee—behind closed doors. An organization's spending plan has its best effect when its creation is a shared experience. All of the key stakeholders deserve to be part of the discussion. The Administrative Board or Council, not a solitary member or committee (including the finance committee), becomes the final arbiter of how the church will steward its resources. Broad budgeting wisdom yields deep ministry impact.

Types of Funds

The categories into which not-for-profit funds are placed are generally three: *restricted, unrestricted,* and *temporarily restricted.* Most general income falls into the unrestricted area in that the monies are gifted unconditionally. The donor assumes the gifts will be used at the organization's discretion for the needs prioritized by its leadership. Offerings to a building fund, or for some similarly designated purpose, qualify as restricted income. The gifts are given with very clear expectations that the funds will serve a particular purpose and none other. Should the purpose for which the gifts were given cease to exist, the organization is required to return the funds to the donors or to negotiate an alternative use endorsed by the donor and the church. Monies given to a church might fall into the temporarily restricted category if the intent is to sequester the income for a short-term purpose. A church might designate a fund for furnishing a new building with the clear instruction that as of a certain date, any remainder in that account will flow into the building fund. Or, the parachurch might create a scholarship fund for a particular category of staff until that category no longer exists, after which any remainder would go to operating expenses. As long as the gift's designation is valid under the organization's structure, that designation must be honored. Otherwise, the gift must either be returned or the donor must agree to allow the gift to be used for alternative purposes.

State and federal regulations expect organizations to abide by the donor's intent. The Association of Fundraising Professionals reflects the spirit of those regulations in its "Donor Bill of Rights."[3] To build trust with not-for-profit organizations, donors have the right to know that their gifts will be used for the purposes for which they were given. To do otherwise equates to misappropriation of funds, a felony offense under the law.

The designations of restricted funds are put in place by the organization, not the donor. The restriction must be defined by an official body within the church or parachurch and then made public before gifts can be assigned as such. The organization has the right to remove the restriction from a fund at its discretion as long as it then returns and/or renegotiates with the donors represented in that pool of income. Many congregations will publicize particular types of giving, for example, operations, missions, building, scholarships, and so on. That leaves the labels generic enough that a wide range of donors can find a place to invest that aligns with their passions.

Managing the Budget

Most congregations have a committee of wise leaders responsible for overseeing the finances. The group usually includes the financial secretary, who relates to the counting team and produces donor contribution statements. When a pastor wants to know how giving is going, the financial secretary has all the information. Also on the finance committee is the church treasurer, who signs the church checks. She or he processes the requests for payment and billing statements according to the approved church budget. The treasurer or the finance chair also produces the monthly financial statements to report the fiscal health of the congregation. The finance committee might also include the board or council chair, a stewardship chairperson, and a chairperson from the personnel committee. It will have a member who oversees the annual auditing function of the church. If the church is larger, the committee will also have an investments team representative and possibly a representative from the church's charitable foundation.

Since most congregations and some parachurches depend on multiple unpaid staff to do the ministry, the finance committee will need to formalize processes and systems for managing the budget. There will be clearly communicated protocols for gaining approval for any purchases made on behalf of the church and how to use the church's tax-exempt number to save that extra expense. This purchase order form will include all of the pertinent information so a leader can buy within the boundaries of church policy and without jeopardizing the congregation's spending priorities. There will be another series of steps to follow to seek repayment for purchases using a request for payment (or request for reimbursement) form. There may be another set of procedures to arrange for travel reimbursement. All three processes would require clear documentation of expenses, including original receipts and mileage logs. Generally Accepted Accounting Principles (GAAP) assume every expenditure can be matched to self-explanatory documents.

The likelihood of unpaid staff being intimately involved in expending financial resources requires some path for communicating when income is lagging and, therefore, spending should be slowed until cash flow improves. The financial need can be shared and expenditures can be curtailed. Most churches can operate with a minimum of one month's worth of expenses in the checking account, if the pastor and leaders are able to capture the attention of the congregation around pressing financial needs on Sunday mornings. For those less inclined to alert the faithful in a worship service announcement, depending instead on written or other forms of communication, then two months of income in the bank might be a more prudent operating reserve. That would allow more time to work through committees and mailings to seek additional financial contributions.

One phenomenon that catches some congregations off guard is nonuniform expenses. Monthly payroll and utility expenses are predictable. Annual or quarterly bills, such as taxes or some forms of insurance, can trigger high anxiety over cash flow since the expense comes due once a year or quarterly, usually with a sizable amount to be paid. The ideal budget will encumber monthly amounts for these quarterly and annual expenses to a savings account so no one is surprised when the bill arrives.

Mastering the Financial Statement

Each organization, regardless of its mission, will have a somewhat customized form with which it communicates its financial position. It is not unusual for even seasoned bankers to ask for some tutoring on a company's financial statement, for example. When examining a not-for-profit's financial statements, you will see the broad classifications of revenues and expenditures. For each account that runs along the left column, there will usually be subsequent columns for month-to-date (MTD) and year-to-date (YTD) information. There may be columns indicating the difference, in dollars, between the budgeted and actual period-to-date numbers. There may be an indication of what percentage of the amounts have come in to date. For example, in reviewing an April statement, one might expect expenditures and revenues to be around one quarter of the annual values.

The front of the statement summarizes the main types of revenues and expenditures. The pages that follow provide a more detailed view of the subcategories, possibly to the fine detail of each account under each category. Extensive detail is important for those who pay the bills and manage the day-to-day spending. It is usually better for a little less detail to be used in Administrative Board or Council meetings.

First Church Financial Statement Sample Month

REVENUES						
Category	MTD Budget	MTD Actual	Difference	YTD Budget	YTD Actual	Difference
General Offerings	$20,000.00	$16,259.10	$3,740.90	$160,000.00	$150,875.76	$9,124.24
Building Fund	$3,000.00	$ 3,419.66	(419.66)	$40,000.00	$31,254.88	$8,745.12
Missions Fund	$0	$0	$0	$10,110.24	$0	$10,110.24
Memorial Fund	$500.00	$375.00	$125.00	$4,500.00	$0	$4500.00
Smith Scholarship	$100.00	$0.00	$100.00	$900.00	$0	$900.00
Interest Income	$29.17	$29.17	$0	$0	$0	$0
Other Income	$0	$0	$0	$0	$0	$0
TOTAL INCOME	$23,629.17	$20,053.76	$3575.41	$215,510.24	$182,130.64	$33,379.60
EXPENDITURES						
Salaries & Benefits	$ 12,031.10	$11,360.42	$670.68	$108,280.00	$102,243.72	$6,036.28
Ministry Programs	$1,270.00	$741.90	$528.10	$12,000.00	$ 975.09	$11,024.91

Facilities & Utilities	$5,300.00	$5,917.98	($617.98)	$47,700.00	$51,955.17	($4,255.17)
Missions	$2,800.00	$3,516.62	($716.62)	$24,000.00	$17,440.50	$6,559.50
Apportion-ments	$2,083.34	$2,000.00	$83.34	$17,600.00	$13,450.00	$4,150.00
Other	$0	$232.10	($232.10)	$0	$1529.93	($1,529.93)
TOTAL EXPENDI-TURES	$23484.44	$23769.02	($284.58)	$209,580.00	$187,594.41	$21,985.59
BALANCE	$144.73	($3,715.26)	$3,859.99	$5,930.24	($5,463.77)	$11,394.01

Other Standard Financial Reports

Along with the financial statement, one would expect to see a balance sheet that portrays the assets and liabilities of the organization, what is owned and what is owed. Assets can include checking accounts, savings accounts, estates, trusts, and short-term investment instruments, such as certificates of deposit. Liabilities can include debt, including mortgages, salary taxes, and any payable item, such as rent or equipment leases.

Also included in the balance sheet is a list of designated and undesignated funds. These items reflect how the organization is fulfilling its promises regarding donor intent. These unrestricted, temporarily restricted, and restricted monies assume clear expectations for their use and due diligence in accounting for them.

First Church Balance Sheet

ASSETS				
Cash Assets				
General Checking				
Building Fund				
Petty Cash				
Savings				
Short-Term CD				
Cash Asset Total				
Fixed Assets				
Church Property				
Smith Estate				
Fixed Assets Total				
LIABILITIES & FUNDS				
Current Liabilities				
Federal Tax Payables				
FICA/Medicare Payables				
State Tax Payables				

County Tax Payables				
City Tax Payables				
Accounts Payable				
Health Insurance Withheld				
Current Liabilities Total				
Long Term Liabilities				
Mortgage				
Equipment Loan				
Long Term Liabilities Total				
Total Liabilities				
Fund Balances				
Undesignated Funds				
General Fund				
Undesignated Funds Total				
Designated Funds				
Benevolence Fund				
Scholarship Fund				

Memorial Fund				
Designated Funds Total				
Total Funds				
TOTAL LIABILITIES & FUNDS				

For the day-to-day financial management, an accountant or administrative assistant will manage the finances using various modules on the accounting software package. Bills payable will be entered into the system as invoices, requests for reimbursements, or other requests for payments, including bills. Payroll will be tracked on another module with details on individual salary packages (wage, payroll taxes, deductions for insurance and other benefits, including any housing allowances). Contributions are recorded by the offering counters, and that information can be used to project income and encourage continued support by donors. Many congregations will issue quarterly individual statements of giving, often with a record of what the individual or household had promised or pledged to give, to allow a comparison of intended versus actual generosity. Each of these modules generates its own reports for administry use.

As the various financial systems sync together, the not-for-profit organization operates on an accountable basis as a steward of all that is entrusted to it. Fiscal surprises and potential crises are minimal as the church or parachurch manages budgets responsibly and communicates mission regularly. Generous people rise to the need of a vibrant enterprise fulfilling godly purposes. Healthy financial stewardship practices fuel that generous giving.

Chapter 6
STEWARDING PLACES AND SPACES

Christian apologist Os Guinness describes the call of God as having three facets. We are first called to a *living relationship* with God in Christ Jesus. We are then called to fulfill a *role* in the mission of God, whether as a stay-at-home parent, a businessperson, or some other professional. Finally, we are called to a particular *location*.[1]

God was so concerned with place that humanity was initially located in a garden, a natural setting with robust capacity to live face-to-face with God. In time, the sacred place became the tabernacle and, eventually, the temple. When the temple was destroyed, synagogues became the gathering spaces for God's people. In the early church, Christians met in homes as well as at larger public places.

If vocation is lived out in location at the individual level, then place and space matter for the church. Ministry is lived out at the intersection of who we are and where we are, our often-changing local communities. American congregations are all too familiar with the impact of transitioning neighborhoods. They understand the ease with which people will drive from their neighborhoods twenty or thirty minutes to worship at the church that is so comfortable for them. These commuters might have lived much closer to the church in the past, only to move farther away when the area began to change years ago. There may be very few from the surrounding three-mile radius who worship with them now. In fact, there might be a stark contrast between the worshipping congregation's demographic and the makeup of those living within walking distance of their building.

Whether the church is located in someone's home, in a shopping mall, under a tree or in a grand cathedral, leaders take responsibility for stewarding the facilities set aside for ministry. Believers gather to worship in spaces they can afford and that meet the need as much as possible. In countries where Christian worshippers are highly restricted in their activities, authorities will often block the availability of meeting spaces as a means of control.

Sociologically, our spaces take on meaning and contribute to our sense of identity. How we care for our spaces speaks volumes about us as well. Worship spaces are called sanctuaries to reflect the theological priority of safe spaces in which to worship God. The stewardship of facilities anticipates keeping sanctuaries safe. Too often congregations choose to defer maintenance and tolerate inefficiencies, particularly in times of financial constraint. By doing so, the safety, not to mention the hospitality, of the space deteriorates.

Hopefully, the architecture of that facility matches the setting. In appearance and configuration, the building should reflect the values of the surrounding area. If the area has changed significantly, the match may no longer be obvious. A ramshackle structure in the middle of a historic district is an eyesore. A well-kept meeting place that blends in with the surroundings communicates respect for context. Our buildings need to be inviting.

In legal terms, churches are responsible for the well-being of anyone on church premises. Safety is the church's responsibility. This may include sidewalks, parking lots, and parsonages. The creative approach to assessing the safety of church property is to hire a safety officer from one of the area businesses to walk through your facility. Advice from the longer-trained professional who is well versed in best practices and governmental regulations will be a wise and high-return investment.

This walking inspection will allow the appropriate church leaders—for example, the board of trustees or a buildings and grounds committee—to evaluate the maintenance needs. Are walkways in good repair? Is there easy access, such as via ramps and elevators, to all public spaces? Is there adequate lighting in all rooms? Is there sufficient ingress and egress? Are hazards removed or at least clearly marked? Is there any evidence of chipping paint or peeling plaster? Are outlets protected in children's spaces? Are there any signs of water damage, and does the plumbing appear to function adequately? Is there sufficient signage around the property, including exit and entrance signs?

Along with a safety expert, there is great value in having an inspection by a heating and air-conditioning specialist at least annually. The same can be said for a plumbing and electrical inspection at least every two or three years. Many times this expertise is resident in the congregation. If a church member is used for these inspections, be sure he is licensed and bonded so as not to jeopardize the relationship and expose the individual to professional liability.

Many older church facilities have beautiful stained-glass windows and other ornate fixtures. Most church insurance policies include these decorative elements in the coverage. This coverage assumes that the ornate features are maintained on a regular basis. This may mean that stained-glass windows will require a storm pane. The leading of the windows should be inspected every five years or so. Other ornate building features will need attention to maintain structural and aesthetic integrity.

A growing concern in many regions is attention to energy efficiency. This participation in the care of God's creation provides a strong witness to a theological understanding of what God has entrusted to the congregation. Such attention might include something as basic as recycling bins and tasteful landscaping. The energy savings realized in using energy-efficient lighting and water-conserving fixtures can be significant. Many public utilities will offer rate discounts for these energy-saving efforts. Inviting the congregation to model local sustainability not only on the church premises but also in their homes will have a ripple effect in the community. Going green isn't just politically correct. Creation care is a biblical mandate and a sign of the breakthrough of the kingdom of God.

Many sizable churches have building use policies to help steward the facilities. Such policies are very functional and, when done well, allow the entire congregation and the community to enjoy the building spaces. Of course, the challenge is to make those policies flexible enough that the building continues to be a tool for ministry rather than a museum only used on Sunday morning. Normal wear and tear is a given in a vital congregation. Regular upkeep is nonnegotiable. When church facilities are used for the sake of others, lives can be changed. When they are deemed an asset too valuable to open to others, congregational decline soon follows.

A typical facilities manual should include schedules for inspections and regular maintenance. It will identify who is responsible for each of the building systems, as well as how the status of each building system will be communicated to the Administrative Board or Council of the church. It should include a safety log for documenting any safety concerns that have been identified by staff or parishioners and how that concern was addressed. This safety log should be available in an insurance file in case any claims are issued to the insurance company. The facilities manual should also describe how the various rooms and spaces in the building will be made available for use. Include steps for scheduling the use of rooms and the management of access and care for those rooms. It should also include diagrams of the various floors and locations of the church facilities. A facilities manual should be reviewed every three years and a copy of the handbook will be shared with the insurance company to document the due diligence that can contribute to lower insurance costs.

One of the common dilemmas of shared space is the issuing of multiple keys to the church building. Over time, with the coming and going of church members and leadership responsibilities, dozens of copies of the church key(s) might be dispersed in the congregation. A wise practice is to number the copies of church keys distributed and to sign in and out those copies, even if only on an annual basis. This will help lessen the likelihood of doors left unlocked and church possessions being stolen.

Another important practice in the care of church facilities is an active inventory process of all church property. This can be as simple as a narrated video as a person walks through each room in the church. A copy of this video should be stored off premises and be available to the insurance company. Any new piece of property should be logged and its value added to the insurance and financial records. If the value of the piece of property is over the minimum of a capital asset (this level is set by the church finance committee or auditing committee, often at $1000), the item should be amortized in the church's financial records. Just as a church builder requires a maintenance schedule, so church furniture should have a replacement schedule that ensures safety and hospitality. Deferred maintenance and replacement can create significant problems long-term.

Any major remodeling of church facilities requires approval by either the board of trustees or a buildings and grounds committee. No major construction should be pursued without appropriate bidding processes and spending controls. The scope of the job should be clearly defined, and the individuals responsible for completing the project on time and on budget should be in place. If the remodeling project includes volunteer workers, the church will want to provide proper supervision and safety measures to keep volunteers safe. Keep the insurance company informed of major renovation and additions as well.

The sample property worksheet that follows illustrates some of the information you will want as you enter assets into your accounting software program and/or other records. You will note that the physical location of the asset is recorded, along with an original and current value. Ideally, property valuation is updated every three to five years or when insurance policies are renewed, whichever comes first. These values could be estimated using an amortization schedule, for example, using a twenty-five-year cycle to write off the value of furniture or land. An insurance company can assist with this process as well. Beware of under- or over-valuation.

Every asset should correlate to a section in the insurance policy as well as the asset schedule on your accounting software. If you conduct an annual or biennial audit, your auditing team can verify proper documentation and help provide comparable item costs for the valuation.

Many nonprofits opt for at least an 80 or 90 percent replacement value on assets in their property insurance policies. Often a 100 percent replacement value is provided by insurance companies at very affordable rates. Very few nonprofits can risk less than 80 percent replacement value on property and facilities. It can become nearly impossible to recover from a catastrophic fire or other loss without the ability to quickly replace space and accommodations.

The property inventory should indicate where documents such as deeds and policies are safeguarded. Copies often are entrusted to a safety deposit box or attorney's office. It is not wise to store them in a parishioner's or staff member's home. The documents need to be visually inspected annually.

A sample property inventory log is below. Note that the capital asset level assumed for this example is $1,000. Accounting software typically allows you to set the amortization number of years (twenty-five vs. fifty, for example) and will automatically count down the value of assets for you. Different types of property are amortized at different rates. For example, a computer might use a five-year rate; furniture might be written off over ten years; buildings could take fifty years to amortize. Your accountant can help set the depreciation rates.

Insurance policies will include less obvious items, such as carpet and cabinets, in their full-replacement coverage. Insurance companies specialize in tracking construction costs and actual replacement claims, so they can help bring reality to your estimates.

Sample Property Inventory Worksheet

Property/Asset	Purchase Date & Original Value	Depreciated Value, Date, & Condition	Insurance Policy Coverage & Section
27 pews in sanctuary	October 1956; $10,000	November 2014; $0 re: amortized; good condition	Acme Property Insurance, Section 8, Full Replacement
Sanctuary altar donated by A. Williams family at 50th anniversary of the church	October 2006; $1,500	November 2014; $200 re: 10 year amortization; excellent condition	Acme Property Insurance, Section 8, Full Replacement

Jones Property (10 undeveloped acres adjacent to church; 8734 Main St.); deed located in Peoples Bank lockbox	December 1999; $15,000 cash + $10,000 donor tax write-off	November 2014; $30,000 re: county valuation assessment; good condition	Acme Property Insurance, Section 6, Liability coverage

The biblical account of the building of the temple (1 Kings 5 and following) provides the driving principle in stewarding places and spaces. While God's glory can be witnessed in all of creation, human beings long for set-aside spaces for worship and service. Their quality and craftsmanship matter. As we consecrate them to God, God makes them holy and God uses them to transform our lives in godliness. Locations become sanctuaries and classrooms for growth in discipleship where relationship and mystery intersect in Christian community. In these buildings we celebrate Eucharist. We rejoice and grieve together. We experience the wooing of God into holy purposes. That is why we care for them well.

Chapter 7

STEWARDING FIDUCIARY RESPONSIBILITY

Like it or not, God and the government expect accountability. The trust invested in congregations and their leaders anticipates good management practices. The congregation is more than a gathering of believers. It bears the role of an incorporated entity subject to commonly accepted legal and ethical standards. As importantly, scripture has a few pointers on good stewardship to consider.

As early as the Genesis account, we see God's assignment to be good caretakers of what is entrusted to us. Adam and Eve had responsibility for tending the garden. Throughout the Old Testament, the prophets judged unscrupulous dealings as one behavior meriting divine judgement. Just practices pleased God. Unjust practices angered God. Several of the Gospel stories call for being wise stewards of what is placed in our care. Paul often instructed church leaders "to be above reproach," for example, Titus 1.

For the latter examples, at least, it was not as if the government standards were warmly accepted by the Christian leaders. It did not matter how unfair the prevailing laws and regulations were at the time. The question was not whether the legal standards were favorable or not to the people of God. The Creator's principles called for behavior reflecting holiness and justice. Any corporate expression of God's people should point to God's character.

The congregation, as one of those expressions, is legally established through articles of incorporation as set out in the laws of the state in which the congregation is located. Long-existing congregations should have a file with a document of incorporation. If not, an inquiry with the secretary of state will allow you to determine whether the church is currently active in its incorporation status. In some states, a church's incorporation must be renewed every five years.

If incorporated, a local congregation will also be expected to have a federal and state employer ID number. These numbers are the identifying mark for any reporting submitted to government officials. They also are used in filing monthly or quarterly tax deposits and reports.

Practically all congregations qualify for nonprofit status, usually under section 501(c)(3) of the federal tax code. The expectations of this tax-exempt status include using all proceeds for nonprofit activities. In recent years, some churches have lost their nonprofit status because they have engaged in political activity from the pulpit or through the congregation. If the church is part of a denomination or association, the tax-exempt status might be provided through that umbrella organization. Whether granted through the denomination or directly to the church, the copy of the tax exempt status letter needs to be on file.

The legal status of a worshipping community is represented by a board of trustees or other legal agent(s). These trustees or directors are personally liable for compliance with governmental laws and regulations. They can be protected from personal liability, at least to a large extent, by ensuring the incorporation of the church. They can also be protected by a clause in the church's insurance policy that indemnifies directors and officers of the corporation. As long as the legal body acts with due diligence in executing its responsibilities, the policy will cover the costs of litigation and similar exposures.

A standard insurance policy for local congregation will include property and liability coverage. It may also include some special categories of coverage. For example, under the property section of the policy, there will be endorsements for building contents, usually in a blanket policy statement. The church would need to determine whether property coverages will be at replacement cost (everything is replaced at current costs at the time of the claim) or whether the church will be satisfied with a percentage of replacement cost. Many policies have an automatic inflation clause that insures 100 percent coverage in between evaluations of the policy. Often there will be a loss of income rider that will provide for financial resources should there be an interruption of regular worship, for example, when a natural disaster hits. There are also property coverages for electronic equipment, such as office computers and sound and lighting systems in the sanctuary. The property section should also include protection from theft of money on church property (like the safe being robbed right after the offering) as well as employee dishonesty.

The liability section of typical insurance policies will have a maximum limit of liability. It is not unusual to see a $1 million individual and a $3 million or $5 million aggregate limit. The limits will vary based on the risk of exposure of the congregation. Liability coverage will often include product liability for food produced or sold on the premises, as well as any other product that might be sold or distributed by the church. Liability also includes coverage for breach of contract, personal injury, false advertising, and special events run by the church. As mentioned in the section above, there is often coverage for clergy officers and board members as well as for the use of non-owned vehicles. If there is a school in the church, there is usually a rider for teacher liability, including coverage for accusations of misuse of student discipline.

Optional coverages might include church vehicles and special art objects. If the church is engaged in a construction project, construction insurance would be another important type of coverage.

Because of the complex nature of local congregations, it is advisable to do a risk assessment every year or so. This assessment may be conducted by the church's insurance agent or with the help of another risk management professional. The categories of risk assessment should include insurance, legal status, and other common exposures.

Whenever the church's insurance policy is scheduled for renewal, a good practice is to conduct an organizational audit. There are multiple tools available, such as the McKinsey tool (http://mckinseyonsociety.com

/ocat/what-is-the-ocat/). These audits are intended to perform a 360-degree review of every system in the organization. They will range from assessment of appropriate staffing to alignment with the strategic vision of the church to adequate facilities and risk management practices.

Another fiduciary responsibility is ensuring appropriate policy manuals exist for staff and volunteers. Along with the personnel manual and financial management manual mentioned elsewhere in this book, it is prudent to include a social media policy that defines appropriate and inappropriate use of social media. It is fairly common to see statements posted on e-mail or Facebook that criticize the pastor or other members of a congregation. On other occasions, the Internet might be used for abusive purposes, including the viewing of pornography. Without a clearly defined social media policy, the church may be limited in correcting any inappropriate behavior. It may also expose itself to greater liability should a lawsuit be filed for failing to address such commonly accepted risks.

Congregations are legally and morally expected to protect children on premises in any church-related activity. Standard practice is to do criminal background checks on any person working with children or students under eighteen years of age. Regular training on healthy practices, such as having two teachers in a room at all times, is required. Safe behaviors must be consistently enforced to protect the well-being of our children. The absence of such policies greatly increases the vulnerability of the children and the possbility of tragic abuse.

Another area of fiduciary responsibility includes emergency response procedures. Such contingency planning has become increasingly necessary in a world of active shooters and unpredictable climate patterns. How does the church prepare for a hurricane or tornado? Where are the places of shelter should an emergency be declared? What steps should be taken to ensure the safety of anyone on the premises in the event of an active shooter? What are the standard fire procedures? A basic emergency preparedness strategy, and training of all staff and regular volunteers in those procedures, is part of the stewardship of Christ's mission in the church.

The sample emergency procedures worksheet at the end of this chapter provides a starting point for thinking through an appropriate level of preparedness for your organization. Consider enlisting a team of professionals, such as first responders, insurance trainers, and medical personnel, who can inform your procedures. Once the guidelines are established, be sure they are easily accessible throughout the facility, for instance, at each employee's desk.

One last area of fiduciary responsibility is a church communications strategy. Who speaks for the congregation? How will any staff member or active volunteer respond if requested to make a statement on the record with a reporter? How will emerging situations be communicated to the public? How will the congregation keep prayer requests and other personal information confidential?

As discussed in another section of this book, the safekeeping of all assets, including wills, trusts, and currency, is the responsibility of the congregation. There should be a clear understanding of basic practices when caring for any asset belonging to the congregation. How are estates and trusts received by the church? When might such assets be refused? How much money should the congregation keep in the checking account(s) and what type of investment instruments are acceptable? All assets should be accounted for in an annual audit. And there should be no mystery as to where those assets are located at any time.

It is prudent for every congregation to have a corporate attorney. This person may or may not be a member of the church. Many times lawyers are willing to provide a limited amount of advice gratis. In larger churches, it might be wise to have an attorney on retainer. The use of legal and financial professionals, along with the other professions mentioned in this book, raises the credibility of the congregation's ministry. It also ensures strong systems to support the church's mission.

Emergency Procedures Worksheet

1. How do we declare an emergency?

2. What are the names and phone numbers of the first people to call in the event of an emergency, after dialing 911?

3. Where are the emergency assembly areas around the facility?

4. Do we conduct regular drills of emergency procedures?

5. Are building evacuation plans clearly posted?

6. Are extinguishers and first aid kits easily available and clearly marked?

7. On what radio and TV stations will we announce closures or other emergency messages? Do we have an emergency information line on our phone system? Do we have texting or other mobile service that also communicates in case of emergency?

8. Do we have a disaster preparedness kit, and if so, where is it located? Are there multiple kits?

9. Do we have an AED defibrillator device? If so, where is it located? Is anyone trained on it?

10. How will we respond to the following:

    •   accidental injury

    •   medical emergencies

    •   a bomb or similar terror threat

    •   a major power outage or water contamination

    •   psychological or emotional trauma events

    •   violent criminal behavior, such as an armed intruder

    •   a fire or explosion

    •   hazardous materials, such as chemical spills and blood spills

    •   other natural disasters

Additional Resources for Creating Emergency Procedures

http://safe-wise.com/downloads/EmergencyPlanningGuidelinesforNon profits_001.pdf

http://unitedmethodistinsurance.org/wp-content/uploads/2011/02 /MPM-Preparing-a-Church-Emergency-Plan.pdf

http://www.umcor.org/UMCOR/Programs/Disaster-Response/US -Disaster-Response/US-Disaster-Response

Chapter 8
STEWARDING THE MISSION OF GOD

God has entrusted us with an awesome opportunity. From the very beginning we have been created in the image of God for the purpose of being on mission with God. Through a grace beyond understanding, we have been invited to cocreate within the parameters of the kingdom of God.

It is not enough to participate in God's redeeming work in an ad hoc fashion. No longer is it sufficient to pull the latest business planning strategy off the shelf. We are in service of the Lord God Almighty. It is a divine strategy that we seek to discern and fulfill. Therefore, while we may adapt good practices from multiple sources, joining God in mission is holy work requiring spiritual listening and obedience.

Two practices lay the foundation for living into the mission of God. As people of God, we seek to have a listening heart (see Solomon's prayer in 1 Kings 3). The healthy congregation engages in a rhythm of study, prayer, and conversation to hear what God has to say about their life together. The Holy Spirit is an equal opportunity whisperer of direction. Each person has the capacity to attend to spiritual promptings. The relational incubator of a discernment community encourages those promptings to emerge into missional clarity. Three sources for understanding the practice of discernment are outlined below: *The Missional Leader, The World Café,* and *Discerning God's Will Together.*

As people of God, discernment informs strategy. Listening to the Spirit through each other, the Word, and prayer begins to paint a picture of what is next. Holy imagination yields holy obedience. Listening practiced in a particular context acknowledges current realities while envisioning what might be. Directional maps begin to take shape, borrowing the wisdom of *Holy Conversations* and *Masterplanning*.

Consultants Alan Roxburgh and Fred Romanuk provide a discernment model that invites the congregation to stir up holy imagination.[1] Through Bible study and prayerful conversation, church members seek to identify the gaps between what is and what could be. The question becomes, what would it look like if Jesus lived in this neighborhood?

As parishioners proceed in these holy conversations, ideas begin to arise for conducting ministry experiments. The Spirit seeds their imaginations with ways to behave differently as followers of Christ. As the shape of this new behavior takes form, this new way of being the body of Christ in their context, a pathway emerges and a strategy evolves. (See the worksheet that follows.)

Another process for discerning for the voice of God in a group of people is the World Café model.[2] This conversational approach is less deterministic and assumes that the wisdom of strategic direction resides in the participants. A facilitator sets the context for a series of conversations in an intentionally hospitable space. A small set of critical questions is designed for the café table discussions. Using large sheets of paper that cover each table, participants are invited to focus on the first critical question collaboratively. Everyone is encouraged to contribute to the discussion of that question. Diverse perspectives are captured by a note taker or by the doodling each participant around the table is encouraged to do during the conversation. The purpose is to listen together for viable insights.

After sufficient time to discuss the first critical question, participants are invited to rotate tables, with one person staying and the other three or four participants moving locations. The same critical question is discussed with the new configuration around each table. This allows a compounding of wisdom regarding that question. This rotation might be repeated. Otherwise, the same shift takes place and a second critical question is discussed in at least two iterations around the table. This process is re-peated until all of the critical questions have been addressed.

The biblical understanding of these models of decision making is the concept of discernment. For God's children who listen for the "kol Yah-weh," hearing God's voice takes precedence over human ingenuity or in-sight. The body of Christ consists of Spirit-filled servants, each of whom enjoys the capacity for attending to God's leading through the Paraclete.

Danny E. Morris and Charles M. Olsen summarize the steps toward discerning God voice.[3] Interestingly, they also begin with the need to frame the issue. As a community, the discerners ground themselves in the decision to be considered, shedding any distractions, rooting themselves in scripture, listening for biblical insights, and exploring what God is say-ing from the texts and conversations. As the insights are refined and evalu-ated, the community builds toward consensus (not necessarily unanimity) until the choice(s) becomes clear and the community opts for and rests in the decision. The assumptions include a common commitment to laying aside personal preferences and submission to the biblical insights gener-ated by a community in dialogue.

In an era of *Robert's Rules of Order*, the process of genuine discernment can seem inefficient and the foundation of trust it requires too difficult to attain. Yet, Christian community, once practiced consistently, provides a unique context for discernment. Relational quality triumphs over demo-cratic strategy when we each come humbly to listen for God's direction.

Gilbert R. Rendle and Alice Mann begin in a similar place as Rox-burgh and Romanuk in their planning model.[4] Using the study of scrip-ture and related missional reading, a congregation begins to ascertain God's purpose for the church in generic terms. Then a subgroup of the congregation is selected to conduct needs assessments. Data is gathered using internal and external audits. Additional reading is prescribed to help the congregation frame information they are aggregating. Next, mission and vision statements are crafted according to the biblical precedents and information regarding the context. Out of the mission and vision state-ments arise objectives, goals, and recommendations. These strategies are submitted to the board and congregation for feedback and refinement.

Once consensus is gained around the next steps, action plans are written and measurement loops are implemented as the congregation puts the new plan into action.

Discernment and planning are the two precursors to living into God's mission. Strategic planning, like that described by Rendle, Mann, and Biehl, assumes a certain amount of predictability. Scenario planning, the emerging approach for futuring, acknowledges that we cannot predict contingencies and the speed of change accurately enough to adequately execute the old strategic planning model. Instead, we need to allow for a handful of possibilities (scenarios).[5]

In strategic planning, the organization identifies its needs and how it might meet them. Through a series of deliberations, strengths and weaknesses are weighed against what opportunities might be feasible. Once the options are defined, they are laid out in short-, mid-, and long-range timelines that utilize the organization's assets while seeking to avoid potential roadblocks, all the while pursuing the vision and mission.

Management coach Bob Biehl suggests these six steps (D.O.C.T.O.R.) assure a thorough and inclusive plan that realistically moves the enterprise forward, including a response to the evaluation of the plan resulting in constantly upgrading the planning process, as well as the plan itself. Direction refers to the question of, What do we do next? Organization is the assigning of roles and expectations to participants in the enterprise. Cash refers to the income, expenses, and net assets for the mission. Tracking entails the setting of mile markers to help measure progress toward the new strategy. Overall evaluation ensures a quality control that keeps the strategy on plan. Refinement is the adjusting movements made along the way as circumstances change.[6]

The alternative scenario planning model uses most of the same steps as strategic planning, with the exception of providing one to three (typically) long-range targets, which might be possible given how circumstances change. In a biblical sense, scenario planning acknowledges a dependence on God's leading while seeking to manage the responsibilities of strategic direction.

For example, most churches talk about making disciples and steadily growing. Very few plan to die. In some regions, such as Buffalo, New York, where the population base is declining, growth is more challenging. It takes careful discernment, holy risk, and unusual opportunity to grow large churches in that part of the country. Many churches in that type of setting at least informally acknowledge that they are facing an uphill battle to grow. One of the demographic realities is that they could continue to decline. At the same time, in faith, they acknowledge God is not stopped by demographics. So faithful scenario planning might say, "If in the next three years we are unable to see steady growth, here are the possible steps we can take to live out God's purposes in our church.... On the other hand, if God does the unusual, here are the steps we will take to steward that miracle..."

Often scenario planning reevaluates the circumstances every three to six months to monitor which scenario(s) seems to be emerging and how to be ready for it. Many of the corporations that have written about their use of this approach, such as Royal Dutch Shell,[7] describe a diligent use of metrics to track the scenarios and estimate the benefits of each path in the plan. In a Christian organization, regular discernment coupled with a prudent use of data positions the leader for optimum effectiveness.

Regardless of the preferred planning model, our responsibility is to faithfully steward God's mission in ways that enlist others into it. The remaining pages in this chapter offer one approach to paying attention to the Lord's leading strategically. They seek to synthesize discernment and planning into an executable process. May the Spirit bring great wisdom and commitment to faith-filled risk taking for the sake of the gospel.

Missional Imagination Worksheet

One process for doing strategic planning is to gather key leaders in a study and reflection group that meets over several months. Consider basing the group on a covenant that will include Bible study, prayer, and discernment. Release the participants from any fear of making final decisions. Their role is to listen. They will act as a holy task force and conduct divinely inspired experiments.

Delegate the decision making to the governance team. While participants might be part of both groups, the missional imagination group is for paying attention to the Lord's insights, not the church's "business." The Administrative Board or Council carries the delegated authority of the congregation, and all major decisions should be managed through that appropriate channel.

As the "missional imagination" group learns more about the immediate surroundings and engages in prayerful consideration, informed by scripture and other spiritual readings, what consensus begins to form? Is there a clear community need that emerges? Maybe the insight is a relationship opportunity. What does the Spirit want to speak into the life of the congregation through this discernment process?

Focus the group on reading through the Gospels or similar apostolic sections of scripture. You may opt for a Bible study curriculum that allows the group to gain a better understanding of the biblical texts. Some additional teaching resources to assist in leading a missional imagination group follow. One caveat: this is not to be a study group aggregating only cognitive insights. This is a discernment group ready to learn and enact what they hear the Spirit saying to them.

- *Introducing the Missional Church: What It Is, Why It Matters, How to Become One* by Alan J. Roxburgh and M. Scott Boren (Grand Rapids: Baker Books, 2009).

- *Five Practices of Fruitful Congregations* by Robert Schnase (Nashville: Abingdon, 2007).

- *A Field Guide for the Missional Congregation* by Richard W. Rouse and Craig Van Gelder (Minneapolis: Augsburg Fortress, 2008).

- *Creating a Missional Culture: Equipping the Church for the Sake of the World* by J. R. Woodward (Downers Grove, IL: InterVarsity Press, 2012).

- *The Permanent Revolution: Apostolic Imagination and Practice for the 21st Century Church* by Alan Hirsch and Tim Catchim (San Francisco: Jossey-Bass, 2012).

Ponder the following questions as you begin this journey of discerning the next chapter God has for your congregation.

1. How aware are we of our immediate surroundings?

Using the resources of a local chamber of commerce or a service agency such as MissionInsite (http://missioninsite.com), gather basic demographic information about the area within a mile of your church. Then see if those demographics change when you extend the area to three to five miles of your church. How much do these demographics compare to the makeup of your congregation? What do they tell us about our neighbors?

Once you have a beginning sense of the information, invite small groups of four to six people to prayer walk the neighborhood. (To explore one model of prayer walking, see John Herring's "Prayer Walking: Putting Legs to Your Prayers," at http://pastors.com/prayer-walking-putting-legs-to-your-prayers.) Listen to the sounds. Observe the context. As appropriate, engage in conversation with those you meet on the walk. When you return to the church, ask each other what God wanted them to see and experience during the walk. A guiding question might be, What might the Lord want to teach us about our surrounding area from what we just experienced?

Talk with local school teachers, first responders, social workers, and other professionals to hear their perceptions of the needs around your church. What stories do they share? How would they encourage the church to better serve the neighborhood? (Be ready to receive some skeptical answers. Sadly, churches in general carry a stigma of short-term interest that too quickly fades away. These professionals will question whether your congregation is committed to building long-term relationships and services. They may also resist anything that feels like proselytizing.)

Allow these stories and other information to simmer in the hearts of your leaders. Be aware that this experience is not to demean the robust history of the church to date. The congregation would not exist had not an earlier group of people engaged in a similar discernment process. There may also be some disagreements over how to describe what the group is observing from scripture and for the surrounding area. Be patient in trying to find common language. Honor the wonderful strengths already in the congregation. Remind the participants that this group will stand on the foundations laid by prior saints.

After several weeks, maybe six months or more, assess what the Spirit seems to be teaching the discernment team. What community strengths and assets have become obvious to you? Where are there already significant relationships? Are there intersections of the congregation's mission and the community's needs? Might there be needs that align with God's heart for your neighbors and the church's calling to demonstrate God's heart?

Discernment leads to holy experimentation. Gaining insight is a means to the end of living faithfully. The wisdom God has shared with your group might be confirming. You might be sensing confirmation of how the church is living out God's grace and hope in the community. The next step might be how to do so in flexible ways so as to grow with the community as it expands.

For most congregations, the discernment process yields both confirmation and challenge. Areas of fidelity to God's mission emerge as well as areas that require greater engagement. For example, a church might celebrate the positive value of a food ministry for the neighborhood that provides meals and groceries to financially at-risk households. At the same time, it might discover that meeting physical needs now must mature to empowering those same households with job training to avoid social codependencies.

As your discernment group understands the challenges, begin to imagine ministry experiments you might initiate to meet the challenge in the name of Christ. If job training is an option for increased mission, consider developing a small mentoring task force that would work with one person or family currently benefiting from the food ministry. This task force could partner with the city job retraining agency to leverage existing resources.

Put a timeline on the experiment that includes monthly or quarterly reflection conversations. What is God teaching us through this experiment? Is there confirmation that this pilot ministry is bearing good fruit? Are there other ministries that do it better, and if so, should we join with them rather than replicate an outreach?

These holy experiments are meant to be low-risk, short-term, "toe-in-the-water" efforts to reconnoiter. Where is the Spirit moving, and how might we join the Spirit there? Who in the congregation might the Lord be calling as mission agents for the needs we have identified? Where might others in the congregation resonate with the community assets and want to add value to their impact in the neighborhood?

As the experiments unfold, reflect on them in light of what scripture teaches the discernment group and how those biblical truths are lived out through the unique personality and calling of the congregation. After the experiment has reached its end date, determine whether that experiment is a onetime learning event or if there is enough momentum and fruit that it should be extended. Powerful ministry often begins as a divinely inspired "What if...?"

2. How well does our congregation nurture Christ-followers who mature into mentors for new Christ-followers?

John Wesley advocated for the genius of personal and social holiness as the both-and of Christianity. As Jesus summed up the Law and the Prophets in loving God and neighbor, so Wesley called Methodists to serving the community and world. He also rooted our social outreach in an individual and communal attentiveness to growing in grace. Not only are we helping to spiritually form the poor and marginalized with our service. They are one source of grace to us as well. Service is always joined with spiritual formation.

Making disciples in the twenty-first century goes beyond merely traditional modes. The confusion we experience around disciple making can be so thick as to blur how we define *disciple* in the first place. Is faithful discipleship merely attending church and Sunday school on a regular basis? Is it tithing and regular mission outreach? Is it prophetically confronting unjust systems and structures? Is it practicing the classical disciplines of personal prayer and scripture reading?

All of these behaviors show up in a biblically authentic disciple of Jesus Christ. To paraphrase Wesley's Ordo Salutis, the way of salvation begins with God's redemptive act in Jesus Christ for a fallen humanity.[8] The death and resurrection of Christ for us becomes personal as God's prevenient grace awakens us to God's love for us. God's convicting grace contrasts holy love with our own sinfulness apart from that redeeming love. God's converting grace bridges the gap between our fallenness and God's original intent for us by helping us to believe the offer of salvation in Jesus. This saving grace brings us into a new relationship with our Creator. We are now adopted children of God transformed by divine forgiveness and presence of God in our lives by the Holy Spirit.

For Wesley, salvation does not stop at the moment of conversion. With the Apostle Paul, he calls us to work out our "salvation with fear and trembling" as we grow in grace into sanctification (see Philippians 2:12 KJV). We mature from spiritual infancy to full Christlikeness. We grow in our ability to listen to God's voice, follow God's will, and be made holy by God's Spirit. Our deepening love for God draws us into holiness in love. Sanctifying and maturing grace works both as a process and as a series of point-in-time moments. When we see Jesus face-to-face in eternity, God's glorifying grace completes the transforming work of salvation.

Most congregations do not adapt a thorough understanding of discipleship. Some focus well on the evangelistic end of the pathway. Others accent the post-conversion end with opportunities for Bible study and outreach. In other congregations, a "pre-Christian" person would have no idea how to explore faith in Christ, let alone what to do to mature as a disciple.

How is it in your congregation? What elements are in place to develop mature disciples of Jesus Christ? How does faith get personal for your attenders? Where can they identify the means of grace, both personal and corporate, that position them for growth in Christlikeness? How do the activities and structures of the church foster spiritual maturity in your people?

Just as you did with the external lens, encourage the discernment group (either the same one or a different one) to enter into a season of study and prayer as well as evaluation. There are many models of disciple making. There can be many activities that we may think build our people up in the faith yet fail to have their full influence because we have not made the purpose of these activities as clear as we might.

The goal of this phase of stewarding God's mission is to enhance the making of disciples. Your congregation would have closed long ago were there not a legacy of spiritual formation in your history. Today you have a new generation you want to deepen in their faithfulness. What shape will disciple making take in your congregation today? How will those discipling wineskins stretch to hold the full weight of biblical Christianity in this time and place? How will they be made easily accessible to your people so anyone can take the next step in his or her spiritual journey?

3. Given what we have learned from reviewing our external mission and internal disciple making, where might God want to focus our attention for ministry?

The general mission statement for any Christian enterprise is making disciples of Jesus Christ. That mandate is the God-glorifying assignment for everyone who is in the faith revealed in scripture. The next step is the nuancing of that mission for a specific group of people in a particular locale. It would be unlikely that a social outreach ministry such as World Vision would make disciples exactly as a congregation in northern Nebraska might. The contexts and resources are different. One is a parachurch and the other a church. The object is to "personalize" disciple making according to the gifts and passions of the organization.

One way to begin honing in on a mission statement is to start it with "The mission of (our organization) is to glorify God by making disciples of Jesus Christ for the sake of the world by..." The common categories that follow for a church include reaching out in witness, maturing people in the faith, and sending them in mission. For a missional community, the steps might entail being the incarnation of Christ in a neighborhood, sharing the gospel by word and deed, inviting others to faith, and build-ing a spiritually transforming community that calls others into missional living.

Along with adapting the Great Commission to a particular context and group, allow the discernment work to shape missional imagination that might be captured in a vision statement. If your congregation ac-complishes its stated mission, what will result? How will the neighbor-hood be changed? How will people be maturing in the faith? What social structures will be altered?

One useful resource in developing a distinctive vision is Will Man-cini's "vision pathway" model. Described in his book *Church Unique* (San Francisco: Jossey-Bass, 2008), this model provides a fresh way of defining vision and mission. You can review the model and learn more about the book at http://visionroom.com.

4. How will your congregation align systems and structures to fulfill God's call on your church?

A predictable stage in stewarding God's mission is to turn our atten-tion to the more customary issues of strategic planning. You will note my bias toward scenario planning as a form of spiritual discernment. Henry Mintzberg rightly names the shift from strategic planning to scenario planning in the business world.[9] Life is far from predictable today. Most planning windows have collapsed from ten years to three. While there is value in visioning farther into the future, the conditions on which strate-gic planning is built—for example, a deterministic ability to predict the future—shift too quickly to forecast beyond one to three years. In light of scripture's invitation to "wait on the Lord" (see Psalm 27:14 KJV), sce-nario planning keeps the options open for the Spirit's unanticipated turn.

The discernment exercises we discussed earlier in this chapter mirror the classical strengths, weaknesses, opportunities, and threats (SWOT) analysis. The purpose is to scan the internal and external environments to identify what looks hopeful and what looks challenging. The evaluation of where God has placed assets for mission, both within the ministry and beyond it, seeds hope as we look to the next chapter of faithfulness. Assessing where there may be gaps or clear barriers helps us hear the Spirit on what doors may be open, closed or delayed. While there may be the occasion to allow God to work through our weaknesses, the typical path is to play to the strengths and opportunities and to either build up weaknesses or to defer to others whose strengths would better serve the needs we have identified.

One aid to doing a SWOT analysis can be found on the Mind Tools website at http://www.mindtools.com/pages/article/worksheets/SWOT AnalysisDownload.htm. It provides a helpful grid with questions for probing internal and external realities.

5. What next steps will you take to continue in faithfulness to God's call upon your congregation or ministry?

Now that the discernment work is well under way, a sense of mission and vision is emerging, and there is greater clarity about where God might be inviting the organization via the SWOT analysis, an action map is required. Who is God raising up to fulfill the mission God has revealed? What are the large-scale missional objectives that will move us toward the mission? What goals must be accomplished to meet the objectives? How will we make them SMART goals (*s*pecific, *m*easurable, *a*ttainable, *r*ealistic, and *t*imely)? What are the sequencing considerations and milestones to mark our progress? Be sure to limit the number of major objectives. Three or four high-level objectives per year are plenty. Any more than that almost guarantees confusion and weak progress.

The planning process now moves to the operational level. An inspiring vision that calls out sacrifice and commitment in God's people will disappoint unless there are details on how to get from here to there. Consider an iterative exercise such as the one modeled in the chart at the end of the chapter. The classical adage is to think in terms of *dime, time, people,* and *places.* Who will do *what* by *when* for *what purpose* utilizing *what monies, spaces, and other resources?*

91

Short-term and long-term sequencing of the goals will allow the allocation of people and resources in a sustainable way. The trajectory of the objectives will guide who needs to be added to the team or repositioned for mission effectiveness. Budgets can be built that serve the mission. This may require some reallocation of facility space and/or financial assets to better serve the strategic need.

The critical step for completing the discernment and planning process is evaluation. Since the goals will be made measurable and tracked by due date, it will be relatively easy to know how or if goals are accomplished. More important is the question of whether the goals are accomplishing the mission. To use foundation grant language, it is not enough to measure outputs like activities and programs. One must evaluate whether or not there are measurable changes in those served—in other words, there need to be outcomes as well. How will the people we serve be changed by what we do and say? How will we know to what degree change has happened in their lives?

Every organization can point to the programs and activities it has completed. Worship occurs every weekend for congregations. How will we know to what degree the participants are worshipping? Christian education offerings are well attended. How will we know that learning, not just teaching, has taken place? What will be the indicators that participants are maturing as disciples?

The by-product of evaluation is improvement. As we learn what is having the desired impact and what is not, we change our strategies to seek a greater impact within the framework of the context and available resources. The Spirit often speaks through prayerfully considered feedback. Discernment includes attending to the "signs," even those rising from evaluating the effects of our ministries.

The mission of God compels us to diligent stewardship. Listening hearts are entrusted with holy imagination for what God might purpose for the organization. Wise, albeit at times imperfect, follow-through on the insights God plants in our hearts breeds faithfulness. Hearing God's voice plus pursuing God's purposes results in seeing God's miracles. Healthy stewardship of God's mission never disappoints. Enjoy the adventure!

Visioning Worksheet

Mission: To glorify God by making disciples of Jesus Christ by…

Vision: Which will result in . . .

    1.   In our congregation:

    2.   In our community:

    3.   Around our region:

    4.   Around the world:

Context: Given what we have discerned about who we are and where God has placed us, we know the following about our context:

    1.

    2.

    3.

    4.

Missional Objectives: To fulfill God's call on our congregation, we will: (Missional Objective #1)

SMART Goals	Timelines	People	Resources
Goal #1.1:			
Goal #1.2:			
Goal #1.3:			

Missional Objectives: To fulfill God's call on our congregation, we will: (Missional Objective #2)

SMART Goals	Timelines	People	Resources
Goal #2.1:			
Goal #2.2:			
Goal #2.3:			

Missional Objectives: To fulfill God's call on our congregation, we will: (Missional Objective #3)			
SMART Goals	Timelines	People	Resources
Goal #3.1:			
Goal #3.2:			
Goal #3.3:			

NOTES

1. The Genius of Administry

1. See Alan Roxburgh and Fred Romanuk, *The Missional Leader: Equipping Your Church to Reach a Changing World* (San Francisco: Jossey-Bass, 2006); and David K. Hurst, *Crisis and Renewal: Meeting the Challenge of Organizational Change* (Harvard Business Review Press, 2002).

2. See "Leadership in the Life Cycle: George Bullard: The Columbia Partnership" (Baptist General Association of Virginia, n.d.), slides, 51 frames, http://slideplayer.com /slide/4267542/, fr. 4.

3. Tom Paterson, *Living the Life You Were Meant to Live* (Saddleback, CA: Purpose Driven Books, 2005).

4. Janet Hagberg, *Real Power: Stages of Personal Power in Organizations*, 3rd ed. (Salem, WI: Sheffield, 2003).

5. Tom Rath, *StrengthsFinder 2.0* (Gallup Press, 2007).

6. http://www.eiconsortium.org/measures/eci_360.html.

2. A Reason for Being

1. See Howard A. Snyder with Daniel V. Runyon, *Decoding the Church: Mapping the DNA of Christ's Body* (Grand Rapids: Baker, 2002), 22ff.

2. See, for example, Jeremiah 15:15 KJV; Romans 2:4 KJV; et al.

3. Stewarding People

1. See Darrell Guder, *The Continuing Conversion of the Church* (Grand Rapids: Eerdmans, 2000).

2. See Robert Schnase, *Five Practices of Fruitful Congregations* (Nashville: Abingdon, 2007).

3. See Wouter Aghina, Marc de Jong, and Daniel Simon, "How the Best Labs Manage Talent," *McKinsey Quarterly*, May 2011, http://www.mckinsey.com/business-functions /organization/our-insights/how-the-best-labs-manage-talent.

4. See Os Guinness, *The Call: Finding and Fulfilling the Central Purpose of Your Life* (Nashville: Thomas Nelson, 1998).

5. Lyle E. Schaller, *The Seven-Day-a-Week Church* (Nashville: Abingdon, 1992).

6. Salary Wizard, accessed November 27, 2016, http://swz.salary.com/SalaryWizard/Pastor-Salary-Details.aspx.

7. See Bill Thrall, in the video clip "How Do You Trust Others and Let Them Love You?" YouTube video, 11:00, posted by Trueface. July 3, 2012, https://www.youtube.com/watch?v=3vsWjIL5sko.

8. See Susan Scott, *Fierce Conversations: Achieving Success at Work and in Life, One Conversation at a Time*, repr. ed. (New York: Berkley, 2004).

9. For a more thorough discussion of personnel systems, see Gil Rendle and Susan Beaumont, *When Moses Meets Aaron: Staffing and Supervision in Large Congregations* (Herndon, VA: Alban Institute, 2007).

4. Stewarding Relationships

1. See Edward T. Hall, *The Hidden Dimension* (New York: Anchor, 1990).

2. Joseph R. Myers, *The Search to Belong: Rethinking Intimacy, Community and Small Groups* (Grand Rapids: Zondervan, 2003).

3. Jane Wei-Skillern and Nora Silver, "Four Network Principles for Collaboration Success," *Foundation Review* 5, no. 1 (2013): 121–29.

4. Ibid., 126.

5. Ibid.

6. See Ori Brafman and Rod A. Beckstrom, *The Starfish and the Spider: The Unstoppable Power of Leaderless Organizations,* repr. ed. (New York: Portfolio, 2008), chap. 4.

7. Ibid.

8. See chapter 9 in Rick Rusaw and Eric Swanson, *The Externally Focused Church* (San Francisco: Jossey-Bass, 2011).

5. Stewarding Resources

1. As stated on the FASB website, accessed June 21, 2011, http://www.fasb.org/facts/index.shtml#mission.

2. Some of the more popular options are Shelby Arena (http://www.shelbysystems.com/products/arena/), CDM+ (http://www.cdmplus.com/), ACS Technologies (http://www.acstechnologies.com/products/acs), and PowerChurch (http://www.powerchurch.com/). For an introduction to the various types of church software, there are occasional articles available on ChristianityToday.com and MinistryMatters.com. There are planning resources available at the National Association of Church Business Administrators site (http://www.nacba.net).

3. See their website at http://www.afpnet.org/Ethics/EnforcementDetail.cfm?ItemNumber=3359.

6. Stewarding Places and Spaces

1. Os Guiness, *The Call: Finding and Fulfilling the Central Purpose of Your Life* (Nashville: Thomas Nelson, 2003).

8. Stewarding the Mission of God

1. Alan Roxburg and Fred Romanuk, *The Missional Leader: Equipping Your Church to Reach a Changing World* (San Francisco: Jossey-Bass, 2006).

2. See "World Café Method," the World Café website, http://www.theworldcafe.com /key-concepts-resources/world-cafe-method/.

3. Danny E. Morris and Charles M. Olsen, *Discerning God's Will Together: A Spiritual Practice for the Church* (Lanham, MD: Rowman & Littlefield Publishers, 2012).

4. Gilbert R. Rendle and Alice Mann, *Holy Conversations: Strategic Planning as Spiritual Practice for Congregations* (Lanham, MD: Rowan and Littlefield, 2003).

5. For more details, see Henry Mintzberg, *The Rise and Fall of Strategic Planning* (New York: Free Press, 1994).

6. Bob Biehl, *Masterplanning: The Complete Guide for Building a Strategic Plan for Your Business, Church, or Organization* (Peabody, MA: Aylen Publishing, 2005).

7. https://www.homeworkmarket.com/content/scenario-planning-royal-dutch-shell.

8. http://www.biblicalstudies.org.uk/pdf/ref-rev/14-4/14-4_colyer.pdf.

9. Mintzberg, *The Rise and Fall of Strategic Planning,* published in 1994, highlights the unpredictability of a fast-changing culture that makes a deterministic approach to planning nearly impossible.

INDEX

CPSIA information can be obtained
at www.ICGtesting.com
Printed in the USA
LVOW13s2033100117
520359LV00005B/5/P

9 781426 727009